P[illegible] Not Found

Published by 404 Ink Limited
www.404Ink.com
hello@404ink.com

Please note: Some references include URLs which may change or be unavailable after publication of this book. All references within endnotes were accessible and accurate as of January 2026 but may experience link rot from there on in.

Editing: Dan Coxon
Typesetting: Laura Jones-Rivera
Proofreading: Kirstyn Smith
Cover illustration: Maria Stoian
Cover brand design: Luke Bird
Co-founders and publishers of 404 Ink:
Heather McDaid & Laura Jones-Rivera

Print ISBN: 978-1-916637-20-7
Ebook ISBN: 978-1-916637-21-4

EU GPSR Authorised Representative
LOGOS EUROPE, 9 rue Nicolas Poussin,
17000, LA ROCHELLE, France
E-mail: Contact@logoseurope.eu

Printed and bound in Great Britain by Clays Ltd, Elcograf S.p.A.

FSC
www.fsc.org
MIX
Paper | Supporting responsible forestry
FSC® C018072

Publisher Not Found

A Decade of Disruption
404 Ink: 2016 – 2026

Heather McDaid & Laura Jones-Rivera

Inklings

Contents

Introduction

Down the cobbled Royal Mile in Edinburgh, past the Scottish Poetry Library and through a claustrophobic alleyway, sits the office where our story really begins. We – Heather McDaid and Laura Jones-Rivera – two reasonably inexperienced freelancers newly employed as temporary digital festival programmers in the early months of 2016, had no idea our lives were about to be tied together inextricably for the next decade.

The office belongs to The Saltire Society, established in 1936 with a mission to encourage and promote Scottish innovation and creativity in the arts. When we began our programming roles, they were seeking to bring their advocacy to a new audience through a virtual book festival celebrating Scottish literature in all its forms on the international stage of social media. While we programmed the event, discussing the books that were pitched to us and their publishers local and conglomerate, the seeds of our own ambitions sprouted.

With a comprehensive background of just-having-graduated from the University of Stirling with Masters degrees in Publishing Studies, and mere months in the industry through internships and assistant roles, added to a history of working for Edinburgh's Christmas markets while posting the weird and wonderful baubles she was selling (Laura) and running a My Chemical Romance fan site and interviewing many a favourite band (Heather), we felt we were the natural bastions to take on the publishing industry with our own brand of youthful naivety.

If I launched a publisher, I would…

If I commissioned books, I would…

It was in the liminal spaces of co-working – the offhand comments about how we never really saw publishers operating in the spaces we occupied online, or comments about how we felt Scottish literary culture was (or was not) represented, or the various crowdfunding campaigns we'd been following (and the gossip – *so* much gossip) – that these conversations, over months, became more tangible. It was, by all accounts, an exciting time. The daydream phase when anything feels possible and nothing is in the way – yet. Then, those speculative "I"s turned to "we".

If we *launched a publisher…*

The true founding of our publishing company 404 Ink arguably took place in a more unusual location: in the company of Sir Killalot. During a day off from festival programming, with a spare ticket to see the revived '90s TV classic *Robot Wars* being filmed in Paisley, we headed off to enjoy some shredded-metal nostalgia. On the drive back home, unable to avoid talking shop, the figurative "if" of the past weeks evolved into "should".

Should we do this? Really give this whole publisher thing a try?

After soul-draining months of half-heartedly applying for permanent London-based, corporate, underpaid, entry-level publishing jobs that we didn't really want had worn us down, knowing we wanted to stay and work in Scotland, our home, it seemed like going DIY was the only way. Based on little experience or idea of *how* to do it, we decided we would give it a hell of a go.

Cosplaying as business owners before we pulled the trigger, we tried filling out a blank business plan template from a random website that asked for a mission statement. With no limits bar our own imagination, we described how we would publish "quality, not quantity" and "publish loudly", explicitly avoiding the growth-centric obsession of capitalist structures while simply publishing books we truly knew should be published with full, undivided attention, growth and profit be damned. We would channel the ethos of our favourite bands and labels who utilised community fandom; we would engage with long-term crowdfunding strategies to bolster our community and income; we would prioritise writing from lesser heard voices; we could build a loyal readership to the 404 brand, who may see us as their literary tastemakers. It was, as we said, the moment for dreaming.

We'd meet at each other's flats and have paper sprawled across tables, the words "business plan" penned amidst a random smattering of words and influences as Luna the labrador nudged everyone for attention. We were buoyed by this energy, the literary peers who we were meeting through the festival, the organisations who came before us and those emerging as we were, and their willingness to offer an hour and some coffee to give us advice as the silhouette of a company came into sharper view.

404 Ink is, in the grand scheme of this illustrious industry, just a speck of dust, but in the years of establishment we were joining a rich history of publishing culture, especially within Scotland specifically. We were greatly influenced by independent titans such as Canongate and '90s DIY publisher and magazine Rebel Inc, who showed the potential for publishing to introduce massively influential and radical writers such as Alasdair Gray and Irvine Welsh respectively, from different ends of the spectrum, from commercial to counterculture. There must have been something in the water in the mid-to-late 2010s, as around 404 Ink's incorporation Scotland saw a boom of new and ambitious small presses such as Luna Press, Charco Press, Speculative Books,

Monstrous Regiment (now Leith Books), Knight Errant Press, and Haunt Publishing, to name a few. Each one no more than one- or two-person teams specialising in their own remits, from sci-fi fantasy fiction, Latin American translation, topical anthologies and literary magazines, queer publishing to Gothic and horror publishing respectively, Scotland's "kitchen-table" publishers were consistently punching above their weight in making the change they wanted to see.

In the wider UK, the big-hitting independents kept coming. Trailblazing OWN IT! began publishing in 2015, expanding into a thriving agency, while 2017 brought Knights Of, the inclusive publisher focused on bringing underrepresented voices to the forefront of commercial children's publishing. The turn of the decade saw this continue with queer-focused Cipher Press, Northern England author-focused Northodox Press, and Scottish comics publisher Quindrie Press. There are so many more who have contributed to the rich culture of UK small press publishing – Fitzcarraldo, Tilted Axis, Penned in the Margins, Jacaranda Books, Peepal Tree Press, And Other Stories, the list is endless. Many of these publishers have gone on to be listed for Booker prizes, industry awards, and are making real, tangible change to an industry that sorely needs it.

As we reflect all these years on, it's an *interesting* time to be employed in the arts. Artificial intelligence threatens/promises to disrupt the way we write, disseminate and compensate information; censorship and tariffs from right-wing international administrations threaten to further cut already wafer-thin margins; and prices creep ever-upwards throughout production processes due to a heady combination of cost-of-living crises from the aftershocks of the COVID-19 pandemic and the ongoing war in Ukraine. Those are just the practical pressures amongst the wider societal issues in discussion today, including arts funding being devalued and consequentially slashed across the world, such as within the National Endowment for the Arts in the USA, as Donald Trump restricts funding for projects promoting diversity or "gender ideology";[1] protest and activism against Palestinian genocide being criminalised and therefore testing the limits of freedom of speech; and the climate crisis threatening our very lives as we know them, with the publishing industry being slow to mitigate its impact.

Still, publishers and creatives persevere. They each had their own moments that made them take the leap into entrepreneurship – some for capital, some for a cause, some just for the love of literature, and others to platform the stories they know are out there, but never quite make it through the commercial process.

On a surface level, the industry could be said to be flourishing – Companies House shows that while 374 new publishing companies were founded in the UK in 2016, 1,530 were incorporated in 2024 alone.[2] The caveat is that many of these companies are sole self-publishing authors and potentially subsidiaries of other larger companies, but it may still indicate a wider interest in publishing entrepreneurship in the UK than ever before.

What we have found on a more boots-on-the-ground, anecdotal front, however, is that small publishers like us just aren't establishing like they did in those peak years before the pandemic, and the ones that are still technically in existence have massively reduced their output and operations, effectively going into semi-permanent hibernation just to survive in the long term.

While it's tempting to use an influx of new companies as a measure of an industry's health, we would argue that it's actually the longevity and sustainability of the companies that truly reflects publishing's prosperity. It is comparatively easy to set up a company and ride the enthusiasm of being shiny and new, but once you have a reputation, a publishing schedule to maintain tied up in numerous other third-party services from sales teams to distributors and printers, and when HMRC comes knocking for corporation tax, the novelty wears off and you're suddenly in the corporate ring, fighting for your company's survival against bigger and more muscly rival companies who have more resources than a small press could even dream of.

If we are to measure the industry's health by the collapse of small independent publishing companies instead, the picture is much bleaker. In the last couple of years alone, we've witnessed the closures of Sandstone Press, Unsung Stories, the aforementioned Knights Of, Quindrie, Haunt and, probably most controversially, crowdfunding publisher Unbound, who left hundreds of authors in the lurch, without any apparent recourse to combat the hundreds of thousands in unpaid royalties.[3] It highlights how easy it can be for a publisher to disappear, whether through mismanagement or inevitability.

A decade on from those late-night caffeine-fuelled brainstorming sessions, we found ourselves asking different questions to the sky-high thinking of our mid-20s. Around 60 books and several hundred published authors later, over 70 award listings or wins, hundreds of pieces of press coverage, many rounds of grant funding, and over a hundred thousand books sold, many potentially company-ending financial external threats later, the question became: *If we closed a publisher, how would we do it?*

The moment came, sitting at one of our dining tables – the noise this time coming from both the same attention-needing labrador and, now, a baby – when we thought about what the next ten years of 404 Ink could look like. After semi-joking about closure, that spark from inception unexpectedly returned. We'll get to the answer to that fateful question in time, and why it felt sizeable to us then; but there's a whole decade to get through first.

As we write, it is a pivotal moment to celebrate the small publishers who challenge the status quo of an industry being squeezed from all sides, who foster diversity, the counterculture, or make their own mark on culture, even if just for a short few years, before many are lost to time. While our publisher cannot be found anymore, the hundreds of others still in operation make up the beating heart of talent discovery, innovative work, culture and community in our country – and, by the time you're finished this book, we hope you will have a deeper understanding of the importance of supporting independent publishers today more than ever.

Running the numbers and using 2023 as an example, 404 Ink's book sales accounted for 0.00089% of the UK publishing industry's £7.1 billion revenue.[4] Our story towards this percentage may not be as compelling as, say, Allen Lane's, who, after visiting his friend Agatha Christie in 1934, decided the market needed affordable books and started the one and only Penguin with its iconic "dignified but flippant" logo; but we still see value in our little 0.0001% corner.

While this book offers a microcosm of the realities of publishing, we naturally don't have room to name check every book and author we've been lucky enough to publish (though you can find a list of them at the end of this book), and we aim to respect their privacy throughout, so any sweeping generalisations and omissions of specific information is in the vein of such protection. We could also write a whole separate book dedicated to bookshops and libraries, to those who brought our books, to readers and audiences beyond our estimations. Independent booksellers are the lifeblood of publishing, while libraries are the lifeblood of communities and should be celebrated and supported to the fullest extent. We mainly want to celebrate what was a monumental ten years for us and to preserve some of the lessons learned along the way before they're lost to time.

If we hoped 404 Ink would truly stand for something in 2016, let this book, a decade later, be our final offering, to depart with the motivations that we founded upon – to publish loudly, with intention, and to share the realities of the industry along the way. It is not our call whether the 404 Ink legacy stands the test of time or not; all we can say is that we sought to stay true to the ethos that galvanised us all those years ago, right until the end.

Chapter 1
Publishing Loudly

Imagine you're in the publishing realm or seek to be. You have a passion for books and writing and want to live a life driven by that passion. The common theme is always that word: passion.

It appears time and again from conference keynotes and descriptors ("a day jam-packed with passion for creative writing and exclusive industry insights")[5] to job application specifications ("A demonstrable passion for books and the publishing industry is essential" says a recent Pan Macmillan role), advice to authors ("If you want to create a lasting writing career, continually pay attention to where your passion overlaps with what is selling")[6] and students ("having an interest in, and passion for the kind of books being published is essential").[7]

While an easy buzzword in an industry where the financial benefits are lacking in comparison to most other professions, "passion" becomes the ultimate driver for success and professional longevity.

Before we fully engrossed ourselves in the publishing realm via internships, jobs, and eventually 404 Ink, our true "passions" lay elsewhere: music. In Heather's early-teen circles, record labels Fueled by Ramen and Pete Wentz of Fall Out Boy's imprint Decaydance Records hosted bands including Paramore, Dashboard Confessional, Panic! At The Disco and The Academy Is…, many of whom were interconnected. The Taste of Chaos tour boasted a dozen-band roster, and the Warped Tour in the USA more so. For her, these were foundational movements in fandom and musical development.

For Laura, the crowd-supported Amanda Palmer was an inspiration (before she grew out of that particularly problematic fandom), while she shared a love for many artists on Reprise Records, formed by Frank Sinatra, which expanded considerably over the decades to include Fleetwood Mac, then Stevie Nicks, My Chemical Romance, Deftones, Black Sabbath, Faith No More, HIM, Joni Mitchell, Mis-teeq, Pvris, Tegan and Sara, The Jesus and Mary Chain, The Used. The Reprise logo was effectively an automatic stamp of approval for us.

Then there's Roadrunner Records, who heralded bands like Slipknot through to Marmozets, with their street team method fully taking advantage of the enthusiasm of fans and their loyalty to their respective bands. The notion of platforming art that a listener/reader/viewer not only liked enough to purchase, or at least obtain, but to actively tell others about through the invaluable word-of-mouth promotion, to then initiate a domino effect for other releases on the relevant label, was already ingrained in us when we put our business hats on years later. We were effectively witnessing the birth of the influencer, though it was less cynically monetised in those days compared to the culture-shaping potential of TikTok virality today. This is how culture met us where we were.

An interconnectedness was present from our seminal years, and our place in music fandoms relied on online connections, where we increasingly saw the labels, the gate-keepers, dipping their toe in to see how fans would respond to a corporate presence. We'd eagerly pick up *Kerrang!* and *Rock Sound* on the newsstands to see the latest news from our favourite bands, and then hop right onto Myspace, Bebo, Piczo and fan forums to gush and gossip. We saw books emerging in these sub-cultures too, a gateway to wider literary landscape. My Chemical Romance was famously named after an Irvine Welsh story, for one, leading to delving into some of his books rather too young, in retrospect.

That direct connection between fans soon became disruptive to the traditional music business, as bands sought to benefit from their connections more directly, either complementing or avoiding their label's involvement altogether. In the 2000s, bands like Mindless Self Indulgence crowdfunded their album *IF*, raising over $220,000 on Kickstarter,[8] and icons TLC raised over $400,000 for their fifth and final eponymous album,[9] where Amanda Palmer crowdfunded not only an album and global tour, breaking over $1 million,[10] but was one of the few creators actively, and successfully, using Patreon – the subscription crowd-funder – before it really took off throughout the artistic scene. The trajectory was clear: connections between fans and creatives were essential to success.

Though we hadn't met until our 20s, these cultural cornerstones had shaped both of our lives thus far, and orbited around our consciousness as we imagined the next stage of our careers. Tides had been turning across the noughties, and being on the fan-end of music, we wondered if we were well versed enough in this dynamic to have a go from the other side, being the platform that sought the fan – the publisher that seeks the reader. "There are a few [record] labels that, no matter what they do, you just trust them," Heather told *HUCK Magazine* in 2017. "We liked the idea of there being an equivalent in publishing."[11] Grandiose as our ambitions were, our experiment began.

First: the what. It's perhaps cliché to say "weird and wonderful", and "stories not often read", but that's where we began. Our shorthand was pointing to Helen McClory (who we would go on to publish) and her debut *On the*

Edges of Vision, a precise and magnificent collection of flash fiction, and say *I want to publish work like hers.* It captivated; it challenged. We also sought work that was "impactful" more broadly – what that looked like, then, we had no idea, but we knew this notion would take shape as we submerged ourselves further into the work.

Structurally, in our early haphazard business plans we stated that we would pay authors over the industry standard (aiming to double the average of 7.5%); we would pay freelance contractors both fairly and quickly (a personal grievance we'd been on the receiving end of) – crucially, we would not pay late. We would have a team page on our website featuring all contractors we worked with, putting freelancers' work on equal footing with any staff. We would share information and hold the door open for others as people did with us. We wanted to generate opportunities for payment, learning, internships and professional growth for as many people as possible besides ourselves.

We would publish with intention and ensure 404 Ink was equally intentional in all that it did and what it stood for. It sounds so simple.

We would decide between us who would focus on the respective elements of editorial, marketing, production, finance, sales and data, and then generally split the rest. Add £12 to incorporate and register 404 Ink Limited on Companies House, spend £149 on ten ISBNs, pay

£250 to a designer for a logo, sign up to Squarespace for a website, and voila. For all intents and purposes, our modest freelance income gave us the means to say we were a publisher. It was time to go into the real world.

In July 2016, we posted simply on Twitter (now X): "404 Ink. Page not found. Yet." This was accompanied by a mysterious glitchy video boosted by the noise of static. Nothing else. Based on this and sparse allusions to launching a literary magazine, people not only followed us, but put down their hard-earned cash in our newly set up Patreon subscription. This was what our conversations had circled in the months building up to our soft launch – we were most excited by how cultural communities operated and fairly monetised their operations. Is that something that could be captured on a smaller scale? Is that something that we can bake into its earliest incarnations? Was there scope to bring publisher and reader more closely together than the larger publishers, who are too big to host meaningful communities for their readers?

The magazine itself was foundational for 404 Ink in many regards. The first issue, *Error*, debuted with over 20 writers, which meant we had over 20 people ready to promote their work to their circles, and likewise 404 Ink – and so fell the dominos. Scotland had a number of long-standing literary magazine outlets, such as *Gutter*;

and an avenue of funding support via Creative Scotland, who would bolster projects that supported writer development and discovery; and a thriving events scene for potential partnerships.

Favouring the literary, the unusual, the alternative, we called for submissions of fiction, poetry and comics, welcoming work in Scots and Gaelic alongside English. There was scope to explore numerous niches at once, forging pathways to new readers, revenue streams, but also author research and development for future 404 Ink publications. Perhaps we'd find our first full-length authors in there?

To speed run the magazine's journey, it did what we set out to do: established the 404 Ink brand, laid down financial foundations to build from, saw us receive our first Creative Scotland grant of around £3,000, allowed us to connect with event partners and reach new readers, and discover new writers. For one, Chris McQueer, whose short story collections *Hings* and *HWFG* we would go on to publish, was in our launch issue, with latter issues featuring a staggering number of writers who would star in our subsequent anthologies and releases, such as Andrés N. Ordorica and Carrie Marshall.

In November 2016, our literary magazine published modestly but successfully, and in December we received our first payout from Patreon, a whopping £322.38 as a result of approximately 30 print and 35 ebook sales from those eager early adopters, complemented by many more sales via our website, amounting to the eventual total sell out of the 250-copy print run. We'd later receive steadily increasing payments for the following magazine issues of increasing print runs via Patreon, until we ended the first iteration of the magazine in 2018.

The 2016 payout was proof of concept, albeit on a microscopic scale. This proof became easier to evidence with the launch of our first "proper" book, the essay anthology *Nasty Women*, which we published a few months later.

In the evening following Donald Trump's win in the 2016 United States presidential election, many lamented online on feeling numb and/or furious that it took a white woman losing the presidential race for eyes to finally open to the systemic racism, misogyny, ableism and general hatred encouraged through toxic branches of American nationalism celebrated by Trump and his cronies. Just a few months after the Brexit vote, UK residents sympathised and feared the rollback of progress on numerous fronts.

While the rise of the right remained shocking for many, for those directly impacted by its injustices over years and decades, this was just another example of their rallying calls not being heard in their true severity until the injustice directly impacted cis, able-bodied white people enough for them to kick up a fuss. Wondering if 404 Ink's first book should engage with this issue, we asked ourselves, *Why don't we reclaim the phrase "nasty woman", used against Hillary Clinton in the presidential race, but offer space on the page to writers whose stories are often sidelined from the mainstream discourse due to the censorious tendency of the far right?*

Here, due to the sensitive nature of the topics we were asking women to write about, such as their lives as daughters of immigrants, as survivors of sexual assault, of their health struggles, their idols, being trans, being politicised for their bodies, their race, class, gender identity and more, we instinctively knew we had to hold ourselves to a higher commissioning standard than the magazine to match the significance of the proposition.

Our mission statement promised that we'd publish diversely, and this was our chance to put our money where our mouth was by sourcing stories rarely seen on the page – a balance of open submissions and direct commissions that saw us broaden the stories we were able to platform – and, crucially, to make those stories heard.

Conceived in November 2016, commissioned in December, launched via Kickstarter the following January to be successfully funded in three days, *Nasty Women* was eventually 369% funded and raised over £22,000 in its first 30-day window. Publishing on International Women's Day in March 2017, it was logical to rush *Nasty Women*'s release to capture a moment in time and prove that crowdfunding a resonating idea for those who want to support both the idea *and* the publisher behind it could be a viable business model.

In the years that followed, politically motivated anthologies were increasingly popular within and outwith crowdfunding, and we saw the success of *On Bodies* from 3 of Cups Press, which explored the varied experiences of the body as a vessel; *Know Your Place* from Dead Ink collated essays about the working class, from the working class; *F, M or Other: Quarrels with the Gender Binary* via Knight Errant Press; and still, today, Verve Books' recent *Someone Like Me*, showcasing non-fiction from autistic writers, carves space for different perspectives from the neurodiverse community.

One anthology that unfortunately did *not* make it to fruition was *No More Mister Nice Guy*, a men's rights response to *Nasty Women* planned by a publisher who wanted to rebuff our feminist output, as we heard via an author friend. To this day, we're sad we didn't get to see that likely tone-deaf campaign fail miserably.

As a publisher, creating inclusive environments where authors know their work is respected and care is taken with their messages was vital. It takes time and experience to foster a space like this – not a one-off declaration but a regular, consistent commitment to this stance through continued work to support, course-correct, learn and improve where necessary. *Nasty Women* was our first one-off declaration, and one that put 404 Ink on the map as a "feminist publisher" – though, we have always contended this label with "feminists who publish" instead, as we didn't wish to be pigeonholed as publishing solely feminist works while we had plans to cover many more topics and issues. It was also our first anthology and our first attempt to fill a gap in the market.

Though hailed at the time as quasi-revolutionaries of publishing for this, we did – and still do – find the praise too easily given. As seen by other companies, publishing "diversely" and "finding new voices" is easy to say in a mission statement, and is a label too easily slapped on projects to avoid confronting deeper, systemic flaws and issues that may plague a publisher (see Stirling Publishing, a particularly egregious example which we'll come to later).

Praise, too, fell on us for democratising the publishing industry through crowdfunding, which is exactly what we set out to be recognised as doing from the very beginning. We certainly benefitted from that in terms of awards recognition and accolades, even if when it arrived it didn't feel as genuine and fulfilling as we hoped, as we worried attention wasn't being paid to the actual books and authors as opposed to our methods of publishing. This raised the overall attention on our publication list, but there are complexities within such praise, wherein authors – often writers of colour – were expected to share, relive and ultimately commodify their trauma within their work for the benefit of readers' needs to be seen to be absorbing "diverse" narratives for their betterment, rather than those authors simply having the space to write about their chosen subjects, whether they include trauma or not. Maybe it was easier to provide critical acclaim for the method of publication as opposed to the more complex contents of the book itself, but whatever the intention, we sought to repurpose any publicity 404 Ink received back to the books at hand.

We do not claim to be the first to run a publishing campaign via crowdfunding, nor to be the most successful. The statistics tell us that on the Kickstarter platform, our *Nasty Women* campaign is, at time of writing, the 8th biggest publishing crowdfunder in Scotland, and 273rd in the country across all categories.

Kickstarter's 470 publishing campaigns based in Scotland pales in comparison to the 6,200 hosted in England, the chasm widening against Wales's 147 publishing projects and Northern Ireland's 87. Maybe it's unsurprising that the most successful British Kickstarter publishing campaigns have been run by companies the size of Verso (the long-standing radical publisher, who faced bankruptcy in the wake of one their distributors' collapse, who raised £322,000 to keep the company going) and even Unbound (whose Douglas Adams archive, *42*, raised £271,000). This is, of course, excluding the global heights of fantasy titan Brandon Sanderson's humble £31 million for four surprise books.

But it's not all about the big names. Dodo Ink, a small literary press, adopted a similar model to our own. *She is Fierce*, a magazine dedicated to showcasing role models and creativity for young girls, was repeatedly funded via Kickstarter; magazine *Marbles* explored the intersections of mental health and culture; organisations ranging from Glasgow Women's Library to publishers Fiction & Feeling and boom saloon were also using the crowd-funding model successfully.

Most notably, and definitely most impactful for 404 Ink, *The Good Immigrant*, edited by Nikesh Shukla, was a groundbreaking 2016 anthology published by Unbound that collected the lived experiences of various writers of colour on what it means to be "other". Navigating the systemic and consistent othering under legacies of imperialism and racism, the anthology featured essays from authors including Salena Godden, Wei Ming Kam, Sabrina Mahfouz and Varaidzo. It was a movement in real time, with *The Guardian* noting it established a "much-needed space of open and unflinching dialogue about race and racism in the UK",[12] before Shukla and original contributor Chimene Suleyman released a new edition in the form of *The Good Immigrant USA*. Graciously responding to our ask as a brand new publisher, Shukla sharing and praising *Nasty Women* at the time was an endorsement beyond our wildest dreams – this was someone whose work we admired profoundly. His endorsement also underlined our responsibility to utilise the trust given to us by our authors, to have their work read, understood and compensated as far as possible. *The Good Immigrant* catalysed cultural momentum, and while the industry still struggles in terms of true equality and equity of experience and recompense, and society has backslid into more overt, dangerous bigotry, the anthology's very creation was revolutionary and should be praised as such, especially as it now receives its second life a decade on at Canongate.

It is this notion of paying it forward, pulling others up with you, that brought 404 Ink to worldwide press, and some money in the bank to invest in further author development. To act as if our trajectory is ours alone is disingenuous. Natasha Onwuemezi at *The Bookseller*, the leading news magazine for the book trade, commissioned our earliest announcements, giving us a legitimacy we couldn't have fathomed even weeks prior.[13] Marion Sinclair, then CEO of Publishing Scotland, offered immediate and comprehensive support throughout not only our formation and acclimatisation, but through to the end. Margaret Atwood, the inimitable author of *The Handmaid's Tale*, supported the *Nasty Women* campaign on Kickstarter and actively promoted it, since taking 404

Ink under her wing with further encouragement over the years. Alan Grierson and John MacPherson, owners of educational publishers Bright Red, with whom one of us worked at the time, provided us with access to their own distribution network so we could be stocked by booksellers, and, crucially, Amazon, to get our work out there on a much larger scale than we could do so alone. Davinder Bedi, who swooped in with the larger distributor BookSource soon after, allowed us to widen our reach across hundreds of UK bookshops and retailers, and has done so for near ten years now. Sharmaine Lovegrove, then Books Editor for *ELLE Magazine*, before being better known for her powerhouse publishing in Dialogue Books, included *Nasty Women* in her International Women's Day article "Books To Read if You're An Activist" alongside bell hooks and Roxane Gay.[14]

It goes on. The Interrobang duo who hosted our first magazine launch event. The writer who submitted to us and circulated the information with their writing groups. The events planner who hosted punk-literary events in London and helped us find our feet there. The fellow upstart publisher who collaborated with us on a book we'd never have the chance to do alone. The librarian who recommended our book gets shelved in their school. The closed Facebook group of new publishers who shared resources. The friend who said, "You know who I think would like *Nasty Women*? Margaret Atwood. I'll tweet her." The publishing executive of a large publishing company in the US who told us, "If you are ever in New York, I'll introduce you to our team." This is just the tip of the iceberg. This is the community we couldn't have planned for yet held us up in incremental ways.

Beyond *Nasty Women*, 2017 became a multifaceted year of experimentation for 404 Ink. We continued to seek publishing loudly via crowdfunding and enthusiastic social media, engaging with as many communities as we could, buoyed by the response to our first year, including being the first ever publisher to top *The List*'s "Hot 100" for figures shaping culture in Scotland, usually saved for the likes of Peter Capaldi or James McAvoy. We celebrated by throwing out free copies of our books to the party's crowd from the stage. (Fingers crossed *The List* had appropriate liability insurance.)

We welcomed the surrealistic Scottish perspectives of Chris McQueer via his genuinely laugh-out-loud short stories, and towards the end of the year we published *The Last Days of James Scythe*, the high-concept fictional accompaniment to rock band Creeper's debut album *Eternity, in Your Arms* that truly allowed us to play in the fandom sandpit. We appeared to be accepted into the UK literary community and became pals with some other like-minded publishers who wanted to promote similar voices to ours, in a similar manner. To see the ethical publishing practices we encouraged not only openly discussed, but celebrated, was our own personal victory.

Despite the accolades, we began to grapple with a new tension that has followed us throughout 404 Ink's time. *Are* we *the people to be doing this? Who are* we *to be doing this?* For one, in regards to the literary magazine, even though we were welcoming and publishing Gaelic fiction, neither of us spoke Gaelic, nor intended to learn. One of us knowing Doric Scots through a rural Aberdeenshire upbringing could only get us so far. We had a very narrow and privileged worldview, in many ways – even more so to take a swing at being a publisher, as if that is something anyone could afford to do. *Is it enough to create the platform, if we personally don't bring a breadth of lived experience to the table? Are we handling these stories with the care needed? What are we missing?*

We've considered this often, and still do, but by this point we were deep in the machinations of publishing and felt that to be here and gaining attention was a privilege, and if we were going to be bold enough to carve the space to create a platform, we should open as many doors for others as possible and do our best to carry that responsibility, even if the path isn't always faultless. For example, we have overstep in our editing, unknowingly let our unconscious biases seep in, and struggled to fully grasp the extent of the journey the author goes through to write from their own lived experience when we are unfamiliar with such a journey ourselves. We have consciously hired freelancers for specific projects to build unique teams that, in the end, we couldn't always support satisfactorily due to being out of our depth as flailing freelancers ourselves. We have had interns come through our virtual doors, only to find ourselves asking afterwards if we truly offered valuable lessons to take forward or if we just bored them with irrelevant half-baked data from our tiny sliver of the industry and gave them £500 for their time.

We often recall advice offered to us by an author at an anthology launch event, which we paraphrase as: "If you're going to do the work, you can either do it or don't do it, but it's not our responsibility to make you feel good about your choice." It was said firmly, in the context of the author being grateful to be part of the anthology we had co-published, and has kept us on track when we questioned every intention yet again. The emotional labour of our choice to be a platform, and who we choose to put on that platform, is ours alone to endure, and we should not be passing this labour on to those we work with for our comfort. It is our job to support them, not the other way around. It doesn't make the challenges and crises in confidence go away, but it helps.

The emotional weight we carry is something underlined further by both the significance of what people were writing about – lives intersected with racism, bigotry and trauma in many cases, or even the mere sacrifices they have had to make to carve out time for writing – and our need to prepare and protect authors as they are sent out into the world. We strove to sell books, but to do so at any cost is not something we were comfortable with. There were some hits we could take – for ourselves as founders, it was the labour of photoshoots and interviews that assumed us to be young and confident girl-boss types for which we had to pretend we were (despite our internal cringing) – but it was a cost we were willing to pay in the hope the press would trickle back down to the authors, as it should. Sometimes it did, sometimes it didn't. Beyond ourselves, we saw the way that press, or the legions on social media could reduce our authors and their work down to simplistic takes depending on their own views.

We have had requests from event programmers saying, explicitly, "Our line-up is too white, do you have any authors of colour we could programme?" instead of approaching us based on author talent. We've seen the tokenisation of working-class writers as a novelty in such a predominantly middle-class industry, and trans writers have been requested for debut panels, despite not being debuts, just to diversify their line-up. We have had journalists egregiously question the legitimacy of an author's autism as part of an alleged review of their book, which we had to request be removed. What is a valid part of people's stories, their own histories, can be reduced to a tick on an EDI form for administrators, or a means of attack scarily easily. We have spoken with many of our authors about these risks during the commissioning process, but remain unsure whether they can truly know what they are agreeing to when they sign up to enter the public arena. For those who do, to say they are happy for parts of themselves to be used as a publicity hook, or a vessel to talk on subjects important to them, can yield good outcomes; it can also reduce them insultingly, or confine them to a thematic pigeonhole they may never escape, or invite people in to weaponise their existence.

Our place in this remains murky, too; we have absolutely hinged pitches to press and programmers on such elements that authors have approved, knowing that this will get a valuable book in front of audiences who would understand and enjoy their work, but we're never fully comfortable about the process. And this is only in a more traditional publishing ecosystem, where we can veto the most egregious outlets; controlling image in a social media climate is a whole other story.

Back in its heyday, Twitter was responsible for around 60% of all our direct online sales, via our website or Kickstarter. It was the centre for profile-building and direct-to-reader interaction; while we will go on to deconstruct these sales versus other routes, this proved vital to our income and the royalties of our authors. It was a vibrant and engaging cultural hub when it wanted to be and was the real source of democratising access to new audiences.

Our latest crowdfunder, in 2024, saw Twitter bring in only about 15–20% of sales, which we believe is more reflective of the platform's downfall at the hands of owner Elon Musk and his rebranding of it to X rather than readers' buying habits, but there is still a case to be made for the sales-benefit of social media platforms today compared to a decade ago. Just look at #BookTok's rise on TikTok, which had at least 1.59 billion users in January 2025[15] compared to X's 586 million.[16] The ongoing push-and-pull is whether or not authors should be on social media, spreading themselves across multiple platforms for additional promotion; we stand firm that no author should be out there making themselves a public figure in ways they don't want. Promotion is firmly the publisher's job; anything else is a bonus.

Sadly, though, we concede – visibility *does* help. SenYinLu, writer of bestseller fantasy tome *Alchemised*, rose through fanfiction circles before their traditional publishing deal saw the work reconceptualised, that acclaim pairing with a (we can only assume) heavily funded publishing campaign to catalyse an established readership; Len Pennie, author of the searing *poyums* and *poyums annaw* poetry collections, has long been known for her Scots Word of the Day series, with hundreds of thousands of followers and viewers primed as potential readers for what is such powerful work. Lucy Rose, author of horror debut *The Lamb*, has cultivated an incredibly strong and natural social brand around herself, that will only continue to rise alongside her work. Established audiences are like catnip to publishers of all sizes, but should never be the overriding driving force.

It's something we saw with our own authors, too – Chris McQueer's first print run of *Hings* sold out before it even published because he was so connected with his audience online, who eagerly read his stories on Medium prior; the second, bigger print run took just a few weeks to similarly fly off the shelves. Elle Nash had grown her readership in America prior to her publication with us, and that bolstered all we would go on to do with her books *Animals Eat Each Other* and *Nudes*. It did not hurt to have the iconic entertainment duo of Forbes Masson, of the Royal Shakespeare Company, and Alan Cumming, currently at the helm of *The Traitors US*, lending their own audiences to the promotion of their book with us, *Victor and Barry's Kelvinside Compendium*. For all these examples, there are others who have no social presences, and their books sold generally well too.

"But social media *does* work for selling books. It isn't shouting into thin air," we'd say on industry panels against publishers who still didn't see the value in it. "We're building a brand that is loud online, and doesn't need every book to stand in isolation to be a success." As the new kids on the block, we had a chip on our shoulder that companies weren't seeing the value in these routes compared with the reach of traditional press and sales channels. We'd talk about it with students, during round table discussions with peers, anyone who would listen. To paraphrase (and butcher) the meme-ified Principal Seymour Skinner from *The Simpsons*, "Am I so out of touch? No, it's the publishers who have been here for years who are wrong."

Many years on, we admit that publishing "loudly" towards sales needs a *little* bit of both, the online word of mouth *and* the traditional sales routes. A number of publishers did underestimate the potential of social media for their brands, and never quite got to grips with it until the world moved on without them. Truthfully, they were also right – to achieve what we wanted to do in terms of our books, to reach the readers we sought, we did have to play the traditional game too, and have a sales team to get us into bookshops for the trade sales that would, eventually, keep 404 Ink afloat more than direct sales via social media could in the long run.

We look back on the *Nasty Women* era, this era where we probably published at our loudest, and there are, of course, elements we would do differently today, hind-sight being 20/20. But for a reasonably haphazard first book (that had a literal typo on the back cover in the first print run, which we only noticed for the first time mid-event, while holding the book aloft for the attendees), it captured the essential intentions of 404 Ink. It was clear to us that publishing successfully, whatever one's metric of success was, was not done in isolation. To only talk about 404 Ink would be a misrepresentation of how publishing was evolving at this time.

This era saw the establishment and flourishing of peers we greatly admired such as OWN IT!, the publisher-now-agency powerhouse formed by Crystal Mahey-Morgan and Jason Morgan, who launched in 2015 with a unique 50/50 royalty model between author and publisher, setting their intentions to be disruptive to the status quo from day one. It was about doing the work, truly. "Let's not confuse the conferences, panel discussions, the articles and the hashtags for action," said Mahey-Morgan in 2017, "because they're not action, they're merely conversation."[17]

"Knights Of was born out of a frustration with the lack of representative voices and narratives in children's fiction," said Aimée Felone, Publishing Director of the inclusive children's publisher she co-founded with Dee Stevens, which sadly went into administration in November 2025. For them, it was always ethos-first. "Books that Matter", a crowdfunder to donate books to children who needed them, launched the organisation before they expanded into their own publishing endeavour, including *New*

York Times bestseller Jason Reynolds, and the now award-winning Elle McNicoll, with a dedication to building an inclusive team behind the scenes, too. "We can publish uniquely, putting our differences first and celebrating them, making it central to our business."[18]

Their crowdfunding has been consistent alongside traditional development, including teaming up with Jacaranda Books in 2020 for their "Inclusive Indies" campaign, to help diversity-led independent publishers tell more stories. "Representative publishing is in crisis," they wrote. "We want to ensure our future."[19] It's now terribly sad to know in hindsight that their future was not ensured, despite raising over £160,000 from thousands of supporters. Again, it is the community that buoys the work. Jacaranda, launched in 2014, were behind campaigns such as #TwentyIn2020, publishing 20 titles by 20 Black British writers in a single year, including Shola von Reinhold's *Lote* and Maame Blue's *Bad Love*. Both publishers have seen award success, being named Small Press of the Year and Children's Publisher of the Year respectively at the British Book Awards in the past.

Other award-winning companies that inspired us include Dublin-based Tramp Press, run by Lisa Coen and Sarah Davis-Goff, who are focused on the small but mighty in terms of output, with the likes of the acclaimed Sara Baume, Mike McCormack and Mona Eltahawy on their roster. Their dynamism as a two-woman publisher reaching critical success stood out, as well as their refusal to read submission letters that open with "Dear Sirs",[20] and campaigning to change Booker Prize submission rules to include Irish publishers. "Because UK publishing benefits a lot from Irish cultural output!"

"We have a fraught history as well, so for greater respect to exist at large, and it's the bigger institutions who fail on that, not our fellow indies," continued Lisa. "Our fellow indies, by the way, are incredibly supportive and generous when it comes to sharing notes and advice. As with anything, it's the bigger outfits that might lack nuance and we hope to be a positive influence on that."[21] Publishing is often coded as "London" due it being the main hub for publishing in the UK, but there are publishers always fighting to remind us that there is so much more beyond the city's borders.

Edinburgh-based Leith Books and London-based Cipher Press both established themselves in the years after 404 Ink's arrival to boost queer voices with a stellar output, while Rebecca Wojturska founded Haunt Publishing to focus on intersectional Gothic and horror. Literary magazines, too, have sprung up: *Extra Teeth*, fronted by a number of fantastic creatives, pay fairly, offer mentorships, and use their space to discuss pertinent cultural topics, such as "Who Gets to be a 'Scottish Writer'?" on division and exclusion within our local literary scene.[22]

"Literature is about speaking truth and reimagining the world," notes Farhaana Arefin, co-founder of Hajar Press, the publisher run by and for people of colour, who focus on tackling institutional racism in the industry. "It's political. If publishers and literary agents really want to fight racism, they need to push beyond diversity and tackle political questions: what structures make us unequal, and how can publishing change society? I see engaging in this struggle as a publisher's most basic moral responsibility."[23]

The aforementioned Shukla truly blazed a trail with the release of *The Good Immigrant*, with subsequent projects of his including the formation of the annual Jhalak Prize for writers of colour with Professor Sunny Singh and Media Diversified, and the Good Agency with Julia Kingsford, though he stepped back as the projects progressed. Though the latter shuttered in March 2025, their parting notes that the agency came about "because we wanted to change two things: for there to be more opportunities for marginalised writers to break through, and for accountability for the industry's shortcomings on diverse publishing to shift, ensuring that no one could say that they didn't publish more diversely because the writers weren't there. We believe we have more than achieved those."[24] The Jhalak Prize continues to grow its awards, spotlighting truly brilliant work year after year.

There is a commonality across radical and progressive publishers throughout the country over the past decade: the push to carve out space, to buoy others' stories. In our case, some experimentation worked, some failed. We wanted to do publishing our way and with our values, above all. It's something Mahey-Morgan noted in her ten-year retrospective on OWN IT! with *The Bookseller*, too: "The only non-negotiable for us is not entering into or staying in anything that doesn't allow us to be truly ourselves and follow our vision the way we feel best in any moment." We see this notion repeated in conversations with peers and presses we've got to know over the years.

For 404 Ink, it was this non-negotiable that kept our mission statement clear, even when external pressures and our own doubts got in the way. The passion that got us here and stokes the fires can often be taken advantage of, but it can also be the signal of the winds changing. This belief, this *genuine* passion for change-making publishing practices that *can* be the vessel for meaningful and sustainable improvement in wider cultural consumption, through publishing *loudly*, with a little bit of dedication and luck along the way – that's the mission.

Chapter 2
The Push and Pull

With our mission rapidly becoming reality, and the reputation of 404 Ink growing, we were transitioning from spare-room side quest into a potential staple of the small publishing community in the UK. The natural next step was to prioritise professionalisation and expansion – a tale as old as time, where business growth equates to long-term success, and we were ready. Not that we had any actual business training or knowledge, of course; we were fully flying by the seat of our pants the entire time. It's a miracle that we led a (largely) profitable company for the time we did. Unsurprisingly, this profit came at a cost for us both, with this unspoken and unseen tension being an undercurrent that runs through the remainder of 404 Ink's history.

In those early years, we were working on various tasks on our clunky laptops at 1am while tucked into Premier

Inn twin beds after a hard day's schmoozing at London Book Fair, which we had scrambled to afford, dedicating every waking moment to growth, to seizing the moment, that elusive next level. Our books were doing much better than we ever dreamed, selling thousands of copies when we only expected hundreds of sales in their lifetime. We had to capitalise. We figured that this is how you run a successful company: through hustle, long hours and trying to sell rights, developing an infrastructure, legitimising ourselves on the wider publishing stage. And quickly. Did we really need to be working past midnight drafting Advance Information sheets for our next publications? No. But we really thought we did and that 404 Ink would be delegitimised if we didn't get this vital email to this essential person by 9am and no later.

The problem is, the hustle and the long hours during 404 Ink's start up were, to an extent, necessary. The moment *is* there to be seized. To offer some extreme tech bro examples, entrepreneur and roman-saluting[25] Elon Musk claims to work 80–100 hours per week,[26] while Apple's Tim Cook rises at 4am to read emails, and Twitter founder Jack Dorsey slacks by getting up at a slovenly 5am before meditating.[27] If it's not about time, it's about attitude: *Love Island* star turned influencer Molly-Mae Hague famously said on the *Diary of a CEO* podcast that "Beyoncé has the same 24 hours in the day that we do",[28] while Kim Kardashian's advice for women in business is to "Get your fucking ass up and work. It seems like nobody wants to work these days."[29] While these examples might work for the privileged white male CEOs of great inheritance, and those whose trajectory is buffered by multimillion-dollar safety nets and globally recognised brands, it cannot and should not be aspirational for those who can just about float the cost of a shared Premier Inn room in central London. There is however, unfortunately, a kernel of truth to the narrative that there is sacrifice when you choose to run a company or work self-employed in the arts. How, when, and where the sacrifice takes place, that cost, is up to the individual.

The standard costs of being a self-employed "hustler" could be listed conveniently as: long hours, lack of sleep, less time spent with loved ones or hobbies, indulging in high-sugar and high-caffeine diets, and attempting to push through the inevitable health issues from all the above. At 24 and 25, these aren't sacrifices that you think about years down the line – if you are able-bodied, missing sleep and poor diets in the mid-20s can be corrected. Well into our 30s, we are still attempting to recalibrate this balance with downtime, and reprioritisation – time and wellness shouldn't suffer to such an extent (we realised a little later than is ideal).

In truth, those early years *do* need dedication and energy to invest in a tight workflow and plan for at least the next three years, identifying funding routes, turnover targets and, in our case, our next publications, especially if sustainability and growth is a target. The lead times in publishing are long to ensure there's sufficient time for editorial development, so critical paths for book retailers are met, and marketing campaigns can be designed and executed diligently. It's both incredibly slow as a process, and fast and furious as a necessary branding exercise, to make the most of start-up momentum and hype. We thought we had to, indeed, "get off our fucking asses and work" otherwise we were ultimately choosing to fail.

Despite our successes, the tensions began to tighten. At the end of 2017, we posted a blog on our website called "We are tired af",[30] "af" meaning "as fuck" – we're showing our millennial ages there, we know. We had spent the year enthusiastically active on Twitter, eagerly tweeting our successes: award-wins; our authors' events and reviews; our headline Edinburgh International Book Festival event with the then First Minister of Scotland Nicola Sturgeon and the incredible Elif Shafak, author of *The Bastard of Istanbul* and many others; our UK tour with Creeper to hand-sell copies of their book at merch stands; all the activities that made for an engaged and curated social media presence. We knew how to make our company look good on social media, and we were good at it. However:

> "Behind the scenes of 404, we are often frantic, frazzled and balancing deadlines in ways that would

make most companies scream, and ultimately, we are learning.

We want to be transparent and straight up say: personally, we have both had quite a terrible year, and we want to give you an overview to underline that everyone is posting through filters and to know that no matter how brilliant or successful they may appear from the outside, there is more going on that you will likely never know about."

Far from a potential 5am rise to meditate, we go on to explain that we had both lost grandparents that year, had various struggles around wellbeing ahead of *Nasty Women*'s launch, even one of our tenement buildings set on fire and necessitated a run through the fire to escape, laying the foundations for some short-term trauma to recover from. We lay out that 404 Ink didn't pay our rent or bills, and that we needed other jobs to make it work. Our work/life balance was non-existent, and we were determined to change it.

It's impossible to look back at this confessional and not cringe, of course, as since then we have inevitably experienced the deeper personal griefs and traumas that come with life, and those initial troubles seem a little small, comparatively. We have indeed developed better "self-care" that we promised to improve as we steered our priorities away from the company solely and towards sustainable balance.

During this period, we were also still seeking freelance employment, as 404 Ink simply did not pay the bills, as is normal for such a hastily founded enterprise with no capital. Being a freelancer is tough, and trying to build a dual career ended up being an unexpected weight added to this survival, with constant queries as to whether we could truthfully dedicate ourselves to a job alongside such a demanding endeavour. We persevered over the years and ultimately found companies who were open-minded to our mental balance, but there were definite years where it seemed the day would never come.

Grappling with these private stresses was wearing over time, and they never truly go away when you're living a double life as entrepreneur and freelancer. Throw in a family to tend to, and now the tension is really cooking. All the more reason for this "professional hobby", as we termed it, to take up as many of our 24 hours, needing evolution into something more sustainable and substantial.

The costs of this "hobby" quickly added up as we continued to mould it around our personal lives. One of us had our first child in 2019, on maternity through 2020 (unpaid, of course); the other balanced this with back-to-back shifts at Edinburgh's Christmas market to keep 404's orders flowing over the festive season. At this time, we also realised that should we both start families simultaneously, we could in no way keep 404 going.

In later years, the unexpected passing of a parent necessitated bereavement leave (unpaid, of course) so the workload again shifted to the other, the balance of babies and book production tautening. By the time a little sibling emerged a few years on, with a second maternity leave (yep, unpaid), the tensions of personal balance in an organisation such as this felt more prominent: the sacrifice starting to feel unfair. One of us is able to have a family, but feels their career stalling and the guilt of not being able to carry as much of 404 as previously; the other has put familial plans on hold for the sake of 404 Ink and carries the workload. The tension furthers when the dedication required to run something of this scale eats away at the potential to expand both of our careers to their fullest potential, our first priority always being to bolster our shared professional backbone in 404. This is no one's fault; but these are the truths of what is given and given up when choices regarding business sustainability have to be made.

While we have tried to grapple with this push-and-pull over the decade, it's inevitable that there are periods of imbalance and resentment towards the opportunities missed or compromised, either from our own actions trying to keep 404 Ink solvent or the wider economic pressures against us. And this is us faltering as a two-person team that is still able to divide the load, to problem-solve together, unlike the many one-person presses setting up that we fear will come up against insurmountable challenges that come hand-in-hand with the isolating experience of entrepreneurship. For our own two-person team, it is both a pleasure to have a business partner to share the journey with, but a curse when we inevitably compare our own personal and professional progressions outside of 404 Ink, and having to come to terms with what can and cannot be ours.

Resentment might be the appropriate word here, and one that is rarely confronted honestly in this publishing industry, that we have seen. Not to be mistaken for a thunderous hatred of every grievance or bump in the road, nor a vehement jealousy of anyone else's success or perceived lack of their own unspoken struggles, but a more low-key, simmering unease tied to the prices often paid through being a small publisher, prices never really seen from the outside. The only time we've seen it explored in an open forum is in a 2024 blog by Jannat Ahmed of Wales-based publisher Lucent Dreaming, as she explores the potential of her small company. The relevant paragraph is worth quoting in full:

> "My question is how to actually *want* Lucent to succeed. Up until now, I've wanted Lucent to stay small. I've wanted it to stay small because Lucent has been a second home for me when my internal life has been chaotic. I've found peace in it being personal. As we've grown though, I've come to resent certain things, like

scrutiny and criticism from careless sources, to people expecting publication deals. I've resented the politics, big and small. I've resented being the site where those politics play out. I resent being so overwhelmed by it all. I've resented making myself quiet or hidden to escape those discomforts."[31]

Without speculating on Ahmed's own circumstance, this really resonated with a lot of what we've privately combated over the last decade, because to complain is indulgent, an issue from the privilege of being self-appointed gatekeepers, the very definition of "first world problems". But we felt it. We too wished for 404 Ink to stay small so we could indulge our other professional ambitions and families simultaneously while allowing ourselves to focus on a modest stable of authors with our full, not-stretched-thin attention. We had been back and forth on growing exponentially and having the pressures increase in line with that trajectory – when we were pushing in the direction of growth, it was because that's the natural capitalist progression.

We also felt the resentment when scrutiny came our way, when we wanted to keep our heads down and just do the work. There was a time we received justified criticism for a poorly conceived event line-up of all-white authors, and others where our overeager editing and hasty justifications to make impending deadlines made us sloppy and careless, causing much-needed conversations with an author where we had to confront that we weren't offering the safe creative space we had promised. Those criticisms stung and inevitably triggered a knee-jerk defensiveness between ourselves that we would *never* intentionally do these things, and our *intentions* should be clear. However, we *did* hold ourselves to a better standard, and, when those standards slipped, we sat with the criticism between us both, really sat with it, and sought to be accountable, and never make the same mistakes again. We had to remember that author who told us to just get on with it, that authors and readers were not responsible for our internal conflicts. That was *our* labour, our mistakes, and ours alone.

But being a gatekeeper, beyond the warranted feedback, seemed to invite a type of vitriol we hadn't anticipated: aspiring authors insulted us when we didn't publish them (a particular favourite is when we were described as being "musty" and like Theresa May. They signed off saying "YOU, CITIZEN OF AN ISLAND." To this day we have no idea what they meant by any of this). A US resident thought we were scammers for charging international shipping and had no qualms in letting us know; or, more seriously, we were sent images of beheaded women for publishing feminist writing or called groomer paedophiles for publishing the memoir of a trans woman. Those examples, while extreme, are symptoms of an extreme Internet culture that we grew up with, and are relatively resilient to. We receive sexist attacks and patronising dismissals regularly but we don't receive racially motivated attacks, or transphobic ire, or death threats. Others, for publishing books that they feel matter, do. If this is what we receive as publishers, we can't even fathom what many of our authors' inboxes have seen.

What we *have* seen is our authors hit with personal attacks in both broadsheet and tabloid trash press, establishments much bigger than our own, leaving us uncertain as to how to combat them on their behalf, if at all. Some of our authors have faced unreasonable legal threats that we had to mediate. Some have led campaign groups or protests to shift the industry in ways that many of our professional collaborators or even other authors disagree with, leaving us, the publisher, somewhere in the middle, unsure how to do best by all parties. These are the varieties of responsibilities of care that a publisher takes on alongside the practical, whether knowingly or not. When you enter the publishing industry just to publish some much-needed books, and get roped into firestorms of varying intensity, it's a breeding ground for tension between the public and private, the "right" and "wrong", the personal and the political.

What we found to be toughest was to publicly engage with those politics, the big and small, when they eventually nipped at our heels. Because we started 404 Ink on such a loud, political note, it has been predictably, understandably assumed that we are politically active and vocal, though we set up the company to represent those who are, and give them a platform, rather than ourselves, until writing this book. We do, however, experience the pressure to be more vocal on behalf of our authors, our collaborators, ourselves, even when 95% of the time we are offline, admin-deep, staring at emails. We too have increasingly found it easier, like Ahmed, to remain hidden and quiet to avoid the discomfort of confrontation or for fear of any backlash that might fall upon us or our authors. We know we can rely on the excuse that we are publishers, not writers, and that we can let our authors do the speaking for us, but that is arguably just that, an excuse, not fully accurate, and not fair on our authors, to effectively be unwitting spokespeople on behalf 404 Ink. A publisher can be a sum of its published parts, but that's not the whole equation and it must have the founders' voice included to complete it, if it is a small, independent, social issue-driven publisher such as we became. In the end, when we consider engaging politically on public platforms today, we ultimately falter when we cannot identify who we are speaking on behalf of – ourselves or 404 Ink.

To resolve this internal tension, we imagine that if 404 Ink was a person of her own standing, she'd fight mercilessly for her values and her allies. She'd never question those values and doubt herself, and she'd never play devil's advocate in the current political hot topic. She'd be at every protest, sign every open letter, promote every GoFundMe campaign. As her founders, we would probably find her intimidating and a little brash, a little quick to anger though her heart is in the right place. We'd envy her confidence and conviction. As individuals we're comparatively meek, often unsure of ourselves, always questioning what is "right" and concerned about doing or saying the wrong thing carelessly, though we think we're generally on the right side of the fence, and seek to always educate ourselves more. We're bad with the words and often find ourselves scattered and stretched thin, which she, 404 Ink, isn't. We find that, in terms of what 404 Ink stands for and believes in, our values are a Venn diagram.

Many people seem to like 404 Ink, the character. They come up to us at events proclaiming how much they admire what 404 Ink does and stands for (which we do very much appreciate) and what they really admire is *her*, not us. While it may seem obvious that a founder is not their company, when a founder invests so much of themselves into its DNA, identities can blur and you don't remember where you begin and the company ends. For us, maybe this crisis of identity is just a symptom of building a public brand in our mid-to-late 20s that we had outgrown by our 30s, while the brand remains in a state of youthful and fighty stasis, unlike us. Now, to decide to close 404 Ink is, to us, to decide to close a door on a part of something that was so intrinsically entwined with our identities for a key period of our lives, but to also bc freed from a part which is locked in amber that stifles our individuality.

While our DNA is inevitably within 404 Ink, so is the DNA of our writers. When we remove ourselves and our own quandaries from the equation, we remember why we set up the company: to platform the best writers out there. They are the ones that make 404 Ink, not us. They are 404 Ink; we – Heather and Laura – are just the compères.

So, where does that leave the two of us? Actually, we're okay. Honestly, we're surprised that we didn't fall out more given all these tensions. We never had any heated arguments, never confronted the other person's bad ideas without caveats and ego soothing. It made us strong business partners, and we knew when to compromise and when to stand our ground. If a bad decision was ever made, it was chalked down to the both of us, never one over the other. As we've discussed, there were times when one was working harder and longer than the other, times where the workload was far from balanced, but as long as the other picked up the slack at some point, scores were not kept. Now, as we work increasingly for other clients, we find ourselves bonded as we lament the loss of our instinctive workflow, knowing exactly who is doing what and that the job will be done satisfactorily, our shorthand communication. Our experiences with other employers aren't always quite as smooth, and we're going to miss the symbiotic balance that got 404 Ink as far as it did.

As troubled as this chapter is, having spent much time on the generally unspoken undercurrent behind many a splashy public face, we think it valuable to include some of the unexpected and often unspoken highs, too. The number of times we've coincidentally seen a stranger in public buying or reading a 404 Ink book. When we've seen some of our favourite musicians actually reading our books and sharing images on Instagram. The times we've unexpectedly come across a title of ours in *Vogue*. How many workshops and talks we've done with aspiring publishers, or schoolkids, looking to learn more about the book world. When an intern has blown us away with their instinct and gone on to a dream role at a big publisher. The moment we open our submissions inbox and see a book that alters our brain chemistry. When a designer submits their first draft of a book cover and it is, unquestionably, the one. The number of days we've needed someone to say "please, take care of yourself" and have refused to work or reply until the other one rests. When we got an email from Alan Cumming asking us to publish a book, and being certifiably convinced it's a very niche type of scam email. The number of times we've picked up books from the printer one hour before a launch event was due to start (no comment) but still made it in time. How many of our authors have gone on to publish at other bigger and better companies and we cheer them on from afar. When we get an email saying our authors have been shortlisted for an award. The number of times a stranger has told us a book of ours reignited their love of reading. When our authors are inducted into the national school curriculum. When we've got to introduce our authors to their childhood literary heroes. When we meet someone who has found any strand of 404 Ink galvanising enough to give their own publisher or project a try.

We're partial to focusing on the weight of the hustle and consequent responsibility that can drag us down, but we also try to hold on to those more fleeting but meaningful moments of what ultimately makes being a publisher genuinely worthwhile.

While the hustle mindset no longer served us from 2018 onwards, the pressure to do the best by our authors and ourselves meant we were constantly adapting in ways we never would have anticipated. Encouraged by the trajectory 404 Ink found itself on, we had a publisher to run and a business plan to draft towards longevity and, of course, world domination via our books. It's such silly bravado that helped keep us motivated when the internal tensions and responsibilities were more challenging. The push-and-pull never allowed for real complacency, or to settle; it was a driving force – both the good and the less so – to move forwards. This whole publishing business lark was a puzzle to be solved; we just had to keep our heads down, and one day, we would make it.

Chapter 3
Survival of the Fittest

The question began as this: how does 404 Ink's 0.0001% (or less, in earlier years) become 0.001%, or – dare we dream – the dizzying heights of 0.01% of the value of the book industry we found ourselves in? Or, if we aren't focused on purely monetary terms, how much space are we are taking up and what quantifies as true success?

The life cycle of a business has been mapped repeatedly in academia across the decades, vaguely summarised as: existence, survival, success, take-off and maturity or decline.[i] It is typically in stage four, "take-off", that a business will professionalise, legitimise and find itself becoming a competitive share of the market that they're part of. Most small and medium-sized publishers will

[i] The life cycle of a small business has been mapped repeatedly in academia since the 1970s, with most models ultimately adapted from a simplistic design of five stages originally theorised by Larry Greiner.

never reach this stage, with the significant majority of such companies most likely floating somewhere between stages two and three, fighting for survival, maybe occasionally tasting the industry's version of success, which can be considered subjective to each publisher.

Success for one publisher may be obtaining the title of Publisher of the Year for their respective country from a reputable awards body. It may be getting TV and film deals for their authors. Success for another may be accelerated growth in publishing widely and commercially, such as with Boldwood, whose profit has grown from establishment in 2019 to making a £2 million profit in 2024,[32] thrusting them through the life-cycle stages at breakneck speed. Ideally, success would be a mix of all these factors, but in reality for the smaller, more social issue-driven publishers, there is a struggle to remain in stage two, navigating the tensions of professionalising without the capital behind us to make it stick. We could talk a good game of our books shifting the world around us, but our decimalised share truly felt huge to us because we were in the centre of it looking out.

We needed more than talk, so we legitimised where we could. If we couldn't turn the success of *Nasty Women* and consequent titles into sustainable profit, we'd instead look to the industry's inner workings and take it from there. The blueprint of what publishing does was there to be followed or deconstructed; we just had to consider what our own metrics and targets for success would be.

One of our targets from the initial business plan was unpaid internships and access to the industry. We know anecdotally that many Scotland-based students have done unpaid internships for a few cornerstone publishers, ourselves included, and that these experiential schemes operate nationally. Such internships have been challenged for over a decade now, from bookcareers.com founder Suzanne Collier saying in 2010 that "unpaid work experience is the scourge of the book publishing industry"[33] to author Kerry Hudson in 2015 calling for such internships to be "banned to build diversity in publishing".[34] It's still the case that those from the working class, disadvantaged and/or minority backgrounds struggle to take on unpaid (or low-paid) internships compared to middle-class graduates.[35] Some say it's simply publishers' "class-induced blindness" as opposed to maliciousness,[36] and we agree – but it seems the only way to correct this imbalance is to simply pay your interns. You can't afford to? Then you can't afford interns. Glib in approach, but 404 Ink's North Star.

It was only in 2017 that new guidelines were published, developed by *The Bookseller* and Publisher's Association, deeming unpaid internships "morally wrong",[37] around the same time Penguin Random House UK vowed to pay work experience participants, not just interns.[38] Initiatives have sprung up since then, from the Spare

Room Project, to the Book Trade Charity's offer of subsidised living for early-career publishers or interns, following the lead of several smaller publishers who had been pushing for this change for some time.

In 404 Ink's early years, even we took on an unpaid intern for a brief amount of time, via a mentorship scheme, more to educate them than to receive labour. But free labour is still free labour and made us uneasy, so we vowed never to do so again, despite 404 Ink, years on, still receiving multiple weekly unsolicited emails from those seeking unpaid work with us. We understand where this desire comes from, but it's a symptom of a costly profession, in more ways than one.

What we experimented with, and would like to encourage the industry to dabble with more, is an openness in what internships can be, beyond their often-rigid forms. Our application process abandoned CVs and cover letters, instead focusing on what professionally motivates the applicant in three simple questions, showing their interests, skills and ambitions outwith the confines of A4 paper margins. The internship itself was flexible, remote, paid and tailored much of the time to what benefited the intern's ambitions and curiosity. The dynamic was different.

This open-ended approach expanded further across our operations as we grew and removed the standard administration from book submissions that are typical in bigger publishing companies, which we emulated before we knew better. We no longer asked for a cover letter, author profile, 50 pages, a plot rundown and one-page summary that includes potential marketing ideas. Instead, we asked: tell us about you, and tell us about your book, in no more than a few hundred words. It gave writers the freedom to share their concise thoughts in their own words without fitting in an onerous process that takes hours to complete.

For submissions for our non-fiction Inklings series, this broadened to: tell us about your book, and tell us why you are the person to write it. The quantities of submissions in every form shot through the roof as the barriers to access dropped, so much so that we eventually regularly received 500–1,000 submissions for every open window. This allowed us to welcome more writers in, and, crucially, understand their work and values better from the get-go, so we knew quite quickly whether they were a good fit for 404 Ink or not. These kinds of submissions numbers were also encouraging to us in that we were reaching new heights of legitimacy, as more writers wanted to work with us. Our promise of ethical commissioning practices and better royalty rates must have been breaking through, and it was time to prove that we could walk the walk, and undertake the extra workload that came with it.

Every discussion of author royalty and income in the UK will likely refer to the 2022 report by the Authors'

Licensing and Collecting Society (ALCS) that states "in 2006, median author earnings were £12,330. In 2022, the median has fallen to £7,000, a drop of 33.2% based on reported figures, or 60.2% when adjusted for inflation."[39]

This might be a shock for the average joe who assumes that to be published is to be making good money, as you may understand through George R. R. Martin's or Steven King's incomes,[40] when it couldn't be further from the truth for the majority. The writing vocation has always carried a prestigious mystique that some within the industry may want to uphold: that the writer is lofty and has the time to write for next to no pay, as their better half or inheritance will cover the bills and the single malts swished from a chaise longue in the writer's office. Today, the industry is generally more accepting that writing is a job and should be paid as such. However, at a £7,000 median income, evidently this understanding is not translating to action.

We believed authors could and should be paid better, and 404 Ink could still be financially sustainable. Our aim was simple: where the standard is an average of 7.5% of RRP for authors (for paperbacks),[41] we'd double it to 15%. For our Inklings authors from 2021 onwards, it would be 25–50% of net receipts, which seemed to be generally unheard of outside of 50/50 profit splits within more radical outfits, such as OWN IT!. Did it work for us? Yes and no, with numerous caveats.

Between October 2016 and August 2025, 404 Ink paid around £180,000 in royalties in total to around 368 authors, across projects. The latest royalty statements we sent to all of our earning authors, from anthology contributors to main list authors, range from the £10 area to the £1,500 range. With twice-yearly royalties, this would still sit far from the £7,000 median that the ALCS calculated in 2022.

Even with our highest earning authors, 404 Ink generally falls far behind the already disappointing standard, try as we might to reach these higher levels. A bigger slice of a smaller pie is, indeed, still a small slice overall. The real structual change would need to be initiated by the Big Five – the five biggest publishing conglomerates in the world: Penguin Random House, Hachette, HarperCollins, Macmillan, and Simon & Schuster – who apparently control about 80% of the US's trade market as a starting point.[42] They are publishing the significant majority of the global market's books, and have the capital and infrastructure to rebalance the scales, should they wish. Our original business plan explicitly stated that we'd prioritise quality over quantity, and this meant sacrificing the perks of regular, reliable cash flow that comes from publishing high quantities. The law of averages says that *some* of those books have to be commercial hits and float the rest of the list, as is the publishing industry's business model, based upon gambling and commodification. 2017 brought us a kind of commercial success to keep 404 Ink's cash flow going, but we knew we needed more in the future for longevity.

Come 2018, partnerships were on the horizon. After a meeting at the London Book Fair with the aforementioned inclusive children's publisher Knights Of, we collaborated in bringing the bestselling middle grade author Jason Reynold's "ode to dreamers" *For Every One* to the wider UK crossover adult market and assist in the hosting of Scottish events across underprivileged schools and libraries. Trusting us, a fellow start-up publisher, with such a beloved and important author was an honour and a privilege that we never underestimated, and the partnership gave us a kind of reputational kudos we were unlikely to conjure on our own.

Closer to home and in the same year, we collaborated with Glasgow-based BHP Comics to publish *We Shall Fight Until We Win*, the graphic novel anthology celebrating the centenary of the first wave of women gaining the right to vote. We worked with the trio of Sha Nazir, Nyla Ahmad and Heather Palmer to bring together the anthology's line-up, additionally allowing us to further stretch our crowdfunding muscles via Kickstarter to raise the necessary capital to bring the book into existence, as BHP led the production and management of the graphic novel and we led the financing and marketing.

These collaborations brought both experience we couldn't have generated on our own, and – again – further legitimacy. Through these partnerships, our books were moving into school spaces we'd never engaged with before, and pages from the comic were displayed in the Scottish Parliament's Holyrood building during a special exhibition – putting political publishing literally on display. This anthology that was modestly crowdfunded was finding its place in history already, all through the merits of collaboration and the sharing of expertise and resources.

However, sporadic crowdfunding could only get us so far, when we knew we had to devise a long-term strategy for sustainability and the growth potential we were still courting. Rejected for loans and grants, we instead found ourselves competing: Scottish EDGE – Scotland's biggest business funding competition, offering grants and loans from £10,000 to £150,000, backed by philanthropic titans like Tom Hunter – appeared on our radar, and despite being the aforementioned meek and nervous types, we applied to present 404 Ink's business case in two categories. Having to do two in-person pitches in a *Dragons' Den*-style[ii] setup had us almost crying and throwing up, with questions being thrown at

[ii] Fun fact: after the grant win, someone from the production company of the actual *Dragons' Den* TV show reached out to us to see if we wanted to apply to be on the programme. After a couple of phone calls explaining the idiosyncrasies of the publishing industry to their research team, *again*, we decided that if they officially invited us to participate, we weren't going to subject ourselves to that level of public humiliation. We'll keep our humiliation private, thanks. (They never did call us back, thankfully.)

us by the panel like "Why do bookshops take so much money from your book sales?" and "Why would you sell rights to your book to another publisher?" With just five minutes to answer, we thought we had inevitably blown it and that we'd never be able to explain the bizarre book industry successfully to an outsider. However, while we didn't win anything from the main pot, we did win the Young EDGE award of £10,000, the only publisher to win an EDGE award, which was quickly spent on rights training, a part-time publishing assistant, a desktop computer and a laptop that could actually run Adobe InDesign without catching fire, the costs in promoting and hosting Jason Reynolds, and, of course, book printing.

It was humbling to see how quickly money could be frittered away in the blink of an eye, with little if any growth to report to Scottish EDGE when they came knocking a year later to see if we had dominated the publishing industry yet. We were still just getting by. It always seemed that we were just a few pounds away from the amount that would click everything into place.

The cash injection bolstered us, both practically and in renewed confidence. As preparation, we put together our most ambitious Creative Scotland application to date and were successfully awarded almost £24,000 for some of our 2018/2019 titles. 2019 became a pivotal year, featuring: *We Were Always Here*, an anthology culminating from the Queer Words Project Scotland pilot by editors Ryan Vance and Michael Lee Richardson that paired established queer authors with emerging ones for mentoring and writing towards the publication; the first UK publication of Elle Nash via *Animals Eat Each Other*; republication of Helen McClory's bizarre and brilliant *The Goldblum Variations* to tie in with our first rights sale to Penguin Random House USA; the debut poetry collection *Let Me Tell You This* from Nadine Aisha Jassat, from which a poem would be added to Scotland's National 5 English curriculum in future years alongside a story of McClory's earlier collections; to name just a few. We also joined a reputable sales team to bolster our sales in bookshops and the trade in general. We were hosting more events with bookshops like the inimitable Lighthouse Books, bringing in audience levels we hadn't seen before. Everything was on the up.

This was also the year we decided to experiment with external publicity campaigns, hiring two different ones to assist with promoting two of our lead titles. Together, the publicity spend was almost £20,000, so we comforted ourselves with old adage of "you have to spend money to make money". While the publicists did manage to garner some light influencer, BBC Radio, and *The Guardian* coverage, these spends did not translate into the sales we needed to make the expenses viable. The books remain ones we are incredibly proud of, but we were still playing make-believe as a bigger publisher than we were – this is what we had been told time and again. This is the publishing game. These are the areas you need to invest in to get through these doors. We kept following that path in hope that the next attempt was the answer.

The fissures really began to show as towards the end of 2019 our dream of professionalising was collapsing around us. Despite having the sales and publicity teams to do the work for our main list of books, where we were unable and lacking their considerably better connected contacts, all while still commissioning for 2020 onwards and reviving our literary magazine with an additional internal 404 Ink team member leading this charge, we were still ultimately failing, as none of this turned into the profit needed to be financially sustainable without subsidy. With these lessons learned, 2020 was going to be better, right?

When the COVID-19 pandemic took hold in early 2020, the western publishing industry was experiencing something of a reckoning. As the pandemic claimed the lives of hundreds of thousands across the globe, those of us working safely from home bore witness to political ineptitude at best and cronyism at worst, with wealth, class and race disparity being fully played out publicly, all amongst the Black Lives Matter movement against police brutality following the murder of George Floyd in May 2020. As many influential figures across media, including literature, posted the black squares of BLM solidarity on social media, author L.L. McKinney started the hashtag #PublishingPaidMe on Twitter to highlight a perennial disparity in publishing regarding the difference in money paid by publishers to non-Black authors vs Black authors. It revealed somewhat predictably that white authors were significantly more likely to receive higher advances than their Black counterparts, indicating a racial prejudice at the core of commissioning practices of those publishers that can afford to pay advances. The hashtag was piggybacked by white authors comparing the money they had earned from publishing with other white authors, neglecting to acknowledge the original purpose of the hashtag and its discussion.

In serendipitous timing, Dr Anamik Saha and Dr Sandra van Lente published the first academic study analysing the UK's cultural production practice and how it disadvantages writers of colour. The report *Rethinking "Diversity" in Publishing* recommended publishers hire more diversely, value and engage better with "BAME" (Black, Asian, Minority Ethnic) audiences, and develop more strategic alliances with writing agencies to reach new audiences and invest in writers of colour.

At 404 Ink, we took the opportunity to assess our own practices in relation to such representation and look at our processes from commissioning through to publication, events, our cultural standing and beyond. We were forced to admit that in some instances, we had actually bolstered the structures we had sought to tear down, such as in author advances: though we could count the number of author advances we gave on one hand, when we did, it was solely to white authors, typically because they were agented with someone to negotiate for them, which white authors are more likely to obtain.

Scotland had its own reckoning with BPOC (Black and people of colour) representation in publishing during 404 Ink's time. In 2019, controversy around the editor of the now-defunct *Scottish Review of Books* swirled as she criticised Creative Scotland's request for them to be more diverse in their editorial practices by declaring Scotland's "ethnic profile" as "patchy and negligible".[43] In the same year, writing for Literature Alliance Scotland, Chitra Ramaswamy, who we were proud to publish in *Nasty Women*, recalled her win at the Saltire Society Book Awards for her non-fiction title *Expecting: The Inner Life of Pregnancy* as exciting, celebratory, a real achievement. But when she was off-stage getting photos done for promotion, she didn't hear how "the head of the organisation returned to the stage and made an off-the-cuff comment about this award really ticking *all the boxes*. It was nothing really, just a light-hearted joke, more at the expense of funders and their infuriating rules than the writer who, did I forget to mention, happens to be Indian, English, bisexual, a woman, the daughter of first-generation immigrants, a mother, and somehow, against all the odds, a writer." Though they apologised for the remark, it significantly stung nonetheless.

Later, in 2021, the founder of Edinburgh-based publisher Stirling Publishing was found to have an open alliance with far-right group Patriotic Alternative, admitting in a public forum to only publishing *Colour of Madness*, an anthology about mental health by BAME authors, "to make money and get nominated for the Jhalak Prize", adding "I wish I'd never done it because I've only had awful anti-white sentiment from all of them."[44]

This is why we return to diverse and inclusive publishing not being a one-time declaration – how easy it appeared for Stirling to publish a book as brilliant as *The Colour of Madness* for one agenda, only to truly, secretly, represent another. We are glad for editors Rianna Walcott and Samara Linton, and their contributors, that the anthology found a new home with Bluebird at Pan Macmillan, while Stirling Publishing quietly closed and disappeared.

Reflecting on these unacceptable comments within the small Scottish publishing and literary community, we return to Ramaswamy's piece suggesting that "diversity is the realisation of quality."[45] This shouldn't be misconstrued as an excuse to dismiss pushes for diversity in the arenas that sorely need them for the purposes of attaining "quality", but instead a celebration of quality inherent within diversity, the quality that weaves a rich cultural tapestry that we should strive for as literary gatekeepers and tastemakers.

This is only further supported by Saha and van Lente in their 2022 study "Diversity, media and racial capitalism", where they identify an "anxiety" in hegemonically white publishing companies as they attempt to publish diversely while still considering books by writers of colour as "niche", and so automatically other the author of colour, who is seemingly never judged by the quality of their work alone as their white counterparts are more likely to be. Saha and van Lente go as far as to say "diversity is a crucial component to the very legitimacy of the modern publishing house"[46] and upon confronting our own commissioning processes in relation to diversity, we reached a similar conclusion and attempted to act on it in the interests of both 404 Ink's sustainability, and the wider literary culture we contribute to.

Publishing often pats itself on the back for miniscule improvements in more diverse storytelling, pointing to these statistics as proof that the industry is saved, though improved diversity in publishing isn't just about the books on a shelf, but the wider culture itself. It's about the longer-tail, where employees are retained and their careers fostered both in the public view and behind the scenes.

Speaking with *The Bookseller* on the stalled momentum in Black publishing as one example, Jasmine Richards, founder of Storymix, said, "The progress is temporary. The movement sparks interest, but then the spotlight fades and so does the interest and investment."[47]

Selina Brown, founder of the Black British Book Festival, added, "What's still missing is deep, structural change. Who's actually in the room making decisions? Who holds the budgets? Black publishing in the UK has so much potential – but it's still being treated like a side dish, not the main course." The discussion broadens more to publishers' focus on individual titles rather than an investment in developing writers' careers, and that behind the scenes, many employees may join the industry, but routes for elevation or motivation to stay in the industry dwindle.

What is needed is a pathway for more lived experiences in positions of power, commissioning, or contribution at the editorial roundtables; freelancers not only brought in as an afterthought, or retroactively addressing processes; but those in control of the budgets and the outreach. There need to be clear routes to publication for aspiring writers where they see similar experiences to their own; a trust that stories and livelihoods are both understood and respected, that needs will be met, and multiple points of view are at the table in all areas – the grant funders, the awards bodies, the events programmers.

To this day, the wider culture faces similar issues about whose point of view gets to shape culture. Christina Neuwirth's 2025 "Quine Report", quantifying inequality in Scottish literature, found that beyond publication skewing to white, male majorities, awards were twice as likely to go to men, and across two national dailies, 82% of reviews were written by male critics. This seeped further into the infrastructure: "the more repeated visibility authors received through festivals, prizes, reviewing and publication, the more Black authors and authors of colour were excluded."[48] This is just Scotland, but we know these issues seep into culture everywhere we look, unless challenged consistently, systemically.

Jumping back to our 2020, we had spent all of our money on our 2019 list and our one 2020 book, Joe Donnelly's *Checkpoint*, discussing how video games can help with mental health. Pivotal as we found this book, and still retain so today, the world was closing down and attention spans were shrinking. Together, we came up with an idea to reinvent 404 Ink's output – a new non-fiction pocketbook series, the Inklings, that would have a 50/50 split of net receipts with authors, would be around 20,000 words total, written quicker than a traditional book to capture the urgency of current issues, and would have a cheap price point of £7.50 to be as accessible as possible for readers. Aware that we were now able to commission in clusters – as each yearly series featured eight books, more than we had before – we could make the explicit effort to commission a broader range of perspectives, writers and topics, particularly as we confronted the equality and diversity gap with more veracity.

Still confident that crowdfunding had a place in publisher longevity, we raised around £16,000 on Crowdfunder for the first eight books in the Inklings series, while Creative Scotland added an extra £10,000 on top as a crowd-matching campaign. This was our most successful crowdfunder, also signalling that funding institutions were exploring support in more experimental ways that could benefit a wider range of projects without the massive application forms to navigate.

The series debuted in 2021, covering topics ranging from the queer revolution of the *Schitt's Creek* TV show and transmasculine joy, to the women ruling hip hop, educating on sight loss, and more. This proved to be a revitalisation for 404 Ink, seeing us adapt and pivot against the wider market's pressure, as COVID continued to strain the ecosystem for small publishers. We observed what the market needed (small, cheap books, a little like Allen Lane's observation in the 1930s – nothing really changes, huh?) and served it. We also moved to a different sales team in the Inklings era, Inpress, who truly "got" 404 Ink compared to our previous one, which strangely negged us in their communications (buy us a drink and we'll tell you that story). Our sales for both the Inklings and our other "main" books started to soar. Survival, for the first time in a long time, was on the horizon.

By 2022, we had our biggest publication year in terms of quantity consisting of Arun Sood's Kavya Prize-winning *New Skin for the Old Ceremony*, Andrés N. Ordorica's debut poetry collection *At Least This I Know*, Liam Konemann's acclaimed novel *The Arena of the Unwell*, Carrie Marshall's brilliant British Book Awards-shortlisted memoir *Carrie Kills A Man*, and six new Inklings, on the topics of death, bereavement, Dungeons & Dragons, personal data and technology, while commissioning further ahead. We were named Rising Stars by *The Bookseller* and won the Saltire Society's Publisher of the Year – we had made it.

...but by December, when we received that latter accolade, we had -£5,000 in the bank account. Indeed, it was confirmed in our annual accounts that year that we made a loss of -£14,000. It seemed that whenever 404 Ink's reputation flourished, its finances languished, and when the money was flowing, the potential was stifling and impossible to turn into real, sustainable profit. We were doing all we had before, but opportunities like Waterstones' elusive Book of the Month promotion remained out of reach; our avenues to press and publicity were yielding fewer results than we needed; editors we'd come to know were leaving their roles for other more lucrative ones, or being forced out in droves. We could never quite get our foot up onto that next rung of the ladder. What were we getting wrong?

With our final receipt of Creative Scotland funding in 2023 – this time to cover the launch of debut author Genevieve Jagger's *Fragile Animals*, bolster the publication of *Gathering: Women of Colour on Nature*, edited by Durre Shahwar and Nasia Sarwar-Skuse and co-funded by Arts Council Wales, and other brilliant titles and authors on our list – we theorised that the £66,000 granted was the ceiling on what we would receive from the public purse and at the limit of what we were comfortable asking for, and that we would be teetering ever closer to our red line of being fully reliant on external funding if we didn't find another route to support us when the book sales alone couldn't keep us afloat.

How do we talk to potential investors, or explore routes of growth, when publishing is not a high-growth industry at the best of times, even for the biggest of publishers? We ultimately realised, over the course of seeking investment in 2023, that to accept investor income was to go against what makes 404 Ink 404 Ink. They didn't sign up to the economic case for the arts being non-excludable and non-rival, nor for the "merit good" argument where books and reading is "so intrinsically worthy that it should be supplied regardless of whether or not people demand it".[49] They wanted to know why we didn't make enough to pay ourselves while we paid freelancers above industry standards; why we prioritised author income over our own profit margins; how the sales of thousands could become tens of thousands of books; how many tasks that we actually enjoyed doing we could outsource to others for low pay, i.e. exploit low-paid labour; how we could supercharge our trajectory to supercharge their investment. A profit-seeking investor understandably ascribes to the best capital-generating models and we struggled to provide this. Their "more" was not our "more".

By 2024, we had accepted that external investment was not an option and our evolution into Publishers with a capital "P" faltered. The chasm between response and reality, personal lives pulling us in different directions, and the increasingly panicked conversations with peers and friends whose own companies or self-employment strained against inflation and increased costs. For us, £160,000 turnover and £1,000 profit in our best year still meant no wages. Counter to our ascension in sales, author reach and accolades, the public and private were never in sync.

We'd been on this merry-go-round numerous times, and didn't know if we had it in us to do it again. We had worked ourselves so hard to get where we were, stage two in the business life-cycle design, but several more years of languishing in no man's land between professionalised hobbyism and profitability seemed less like survival and more like self-inflicted destruction. Our labour of love had its moment and, it seemed, achieved what it set out to do, even if it wouldn't last forever. Maybe we needed to accept that that was enough.

Chapter 4
Show Me the Money

Let us be clear. The finances of the publishing industry are wild. Actually *wild*. We know that when companies talk about successes and failures, what we all really wonder is: yes, but what about the money? Where did it come from and what did you do with it?

No need to wonder – we think it would be rather fun to tell you, in detail, the monetary mechanics of our little publisher.

Galley Beggar Press, another small independent, wrote a piece in 2023 named "What does it cost to produce a book?"[50] where they explain that "the cost of producing a book has more than doubled since 2015", ultimately calculating that after all the other costs of printing, distribution, sales commission, bookseller cut and author royalties, the publisher is left with a profit of £0.43 to £0.93 in 2015, compared with £-0.46 to £0.21 in 2023.

With the huge increase in publishing costs due to reasons exogenic (such as Brexit increasing trade costs for those in the UK; COVID challenging economies overall; the Ukraine war increasing the costs of paper) and endogenic (continually low book recommended retail prices (RRPs) against inflation; sparse review space in publications; shrinking shelf space in chain bookshops for small, independently published books), it's kind of a miracle that small publishers still exist at all. Indeed, the industry is fearful on an existential scale today (and honestly, has always been, as Michael Bhaskar simply states in *The Content Machine*, "Publishing, famously, is always in crisis").[51] An open letter penned by numerous UK small publishers in 2025[52] and signed by us calls for cohesive collaboration between the UK's cultural policy bodies and publishers to identify more essential sustainable support, as one of the most pertinent symptoms in our latest crisis.

By now, you should be well-versed in 404 Ink's approach to ethical finances where authors should be paid more than the industry standard, we pay our freelancers and interns at least living wage, and we, the founders, are generally the last to be paid in the company, if at all. Values and the passion behind them are all well and good, but it's the finances that ultimately deem a publisher successful or not.

As we analyse the finances more closely, we shamelessly steal the method dubbed "clown math" from the excellent gaming industry journalist and streamer Lawrence Sonntag, who adopts said method when there is scant, inconsistent, or assumed data used to extrapolate a narrative, which should then be taken with a pinch of salt. This is how we ask every reader to treat our calculations and consequent conclusions in this chapter. While the data provided is as accurate as possible, figures are rounded up or down conveniently, and averages are calculated with reluctance. Some numbers are missing from changes in systems, some are guessed due to a lack of data from the source. We also make mistakes in our calculations from time to time, and sometimes we miss them. We are not financial experts, we are just publishers doing our best, and nothing herein constitutes financial advice. Let the clown math commence.

Remember that figure that said 404 Ink was just 0.00089% of the UK publishing industry's total revenue in 2023? Keeping that context in mind, while some of the numbers we'll discuss will be in the hundreds of thousands, considerable cash for the average reader (and for us!), this is a drop in the ocean not just within the wider UK industry, but also in UK independent publishing. For example, Profile reported its annual turnover, ending March 2025, as £21.5 million, with its operating profit sitting at £3 million,[53] while Bloomsbury reports £24 million profit for six months of 2025 alone.[54] In

2023–24, Canongate reported a £17.9 million turnover, sending £8.8 million in royalties to their authors/agents,[55] while, comparatively, 404 Ink's turnover was our biggest yet at £166,219, sending £22,396.58 of royalties to authors/agents. Still feeling very humble…

We know we're small, financially, but as a publisher we've always tried to punch above our weight and identify where we can make the most difference in our corner. Upon calculating that aforementioned £180,000 figure we have provided to authors, plus around £60,000 to freelancers, we couldn't help but be proud, actually. We imagine telling our 25-year-old selves in 2016 that we'd contribute a little under a quarter of a million pounds to creatives over the span of 404 Ink's time. We did *technically* succeed at paying our authors above industry average rates. Some authors benefitted when their books really hit the right markets at the right time, selling over 10,000 copies in some instances. But some we did not manage to generate the same success for, sadly. While promising a 15% royalty is big talk, we have to remember that the value of 15% hinges very heavily on the value of the 100%. Some of our authors sold lower numbers than we expected, and their royalty statements sadly reflected that. We didn't turn any of our authors into *Sunday Times* bestsellers, nor did we make enough money for them to make a full-time living from their work. But, then again, neither do the Big Five publishers most of the time. The key here is not to measure your success against impossible industry standards, as we did originally, or else risk a fairly constant diet of disappointment and chasing down the unobtainable.

It was particularly disappointing to realise around 2022 that we weren't going to be able to keep up 50% net receipt royalties for our Inklings authors because they were too damned successful. The intricate financial design only worked if most of the sales we made for the Inklings were direct, via our website, as we intended in the depths of the pandemic. If no one was going to bookshops anymore, they'd buy them online and our profit margin would be plentiful, with much of it going to the authors. They'd be making thousands of pounds a year. *True equity! We did it!*

Then normal bookshop service resumed and suddenly they wanted thousands of our Inklings – but they weren't priced to handle the additional cuts that had to be taken by the bookshops, our distributor and our sales team.

Here's an example of how the splits of an Inkling can work.

The following pie chart shows the splits when a £7.50 Inkling, printed in 2025, is sold directly to a reader via our own website, and the author receives a royalty of 25% of net receipts.

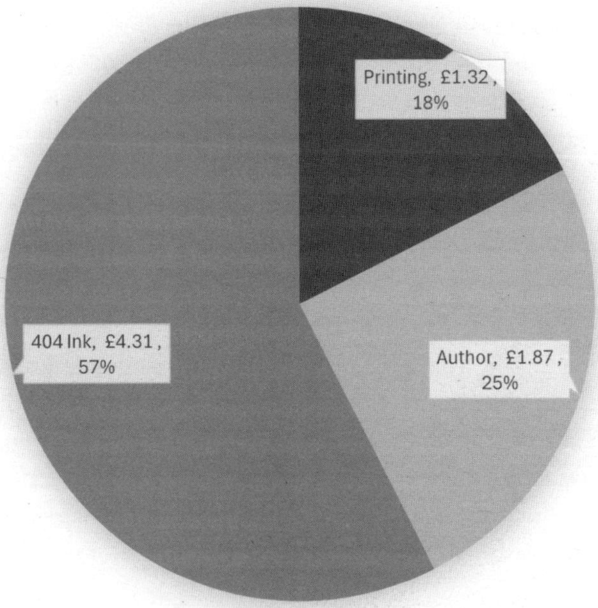

Here, we make a healthy return from a sale via our website, and this is where the authors also get the biggest royalties, because there are no other slices of the pie reserved for other parties. An order comes in, we pack it up and and head to the post office. No distributors or sales teams need a cut. Over the lifetime of 404 Ink, the average order value (AOV) of a sale via 404 Ink's website was £11.17. The AOV of a sale via trade, i.e. bookshops and online retailers including Amazon, was £3.83. We relied a lot upon our website to stay afloat, as you can imagine.

The next chart roughly shows the splits when the same Inkling is sold via a bookshop, when the bookshop buys the book from us at 50% of the RRP, which is the average discount we have to give bookshops.

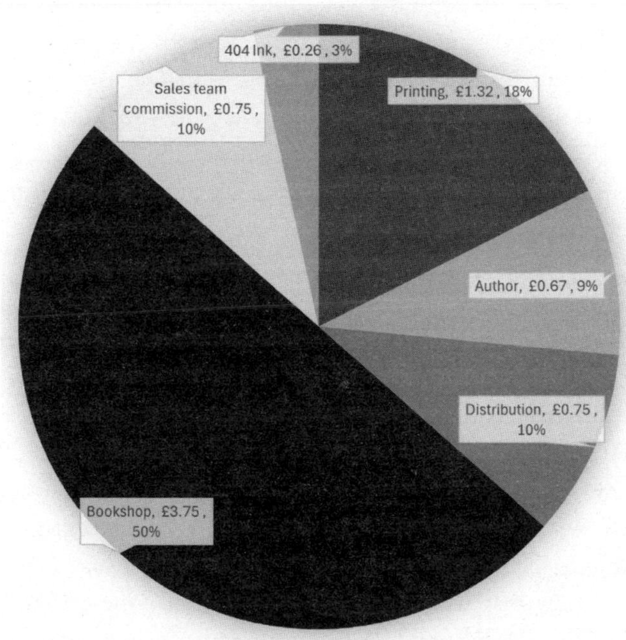

What 404 Ink receives for a retailer sale is significantly smaller, almost nothing, and you can imagine how much worse it was when the royalties we gave to the authors

were double – we were possibly *losing* money on the first Inklings series for a while when they really took off in bookshops across the UK. More similar to those margins calculated in Galley Beggar's article, these statistics might indicate a consistent trend where the unit costs in printing rise and the share for publishers falls steadily. It was increasingly challenging to uphold the promised generous royalties, and so we fell gradually closer in line with the industry standard, sadly. We still provide quarterly royalty statements and payments for our Inklings authors, compared to the typical twice per year, in the hope more regular cash influxes are appreciated.

This is the financial juggle for the authors, but what about the freelancers we promised to pay fairly as part of our founding pillars? We paid freelancers of varying roles, cover designers, rights consultants, illustrators, editors, assistants and so on, as noted, around £60,000 over our time. Simpler than the complexities of author royalty calculation, we're told by our freelancers how much the work costs, and we pay it, on time. Interestingly, that total almost exactly matches the £56,000 which 404 Ink paid to the both of us over nine years, averaging at a little over £3,000 each per year, though the reality was that there were years of zero pay and some years of higher pay, all depending on the level of funding received that year that could cover project-specific expenses. We were constantly juggling other jobs, because no one is living on £3,000 a year, but it's still not quite the sacrifice we set out to take on, to be the last to be paid in our ecosystem. It didn't take too long after the first year or two of ridiculous workload to realise we'd have to receive *some* payment for our work to keep it sustainable. This is when we got serious about applying for Creative Scotland funding – not to fill our own pockets, but to inject the company with the bare minimum to make the books and get them in front of readers. If we were able to make a profit from this, then maybe we, as directors, might actually start to take some payment from the company.

Our estimate is that we received around £140,000 in total funding from Creative Scotland's National Lottery Fund via the Open Project Fund, which is public funding, budgeted and ultimately controlled by the Scottish Government. England, Wales and Ireland all have their own version of this system. The rationale is that anyone, artist or middleman such as ourselves, can apply for funding from this pot for a one-off project. The application is dozens of pages long and can take months of drafting and budgeting before it's ready for submission. We got this rigmarole down to a science by our third or fourth application and received, as we've mentioned, modest funding in 2016 for our literary magazine, up to around £66,000 for our publication season in 2023–25, partially covering around 10 books, internship and career development opportunities and other elements in the process. 404 Ink couldn't have operated as long as it did without this funding, for which we are forever grateful. However, there are some quirks in the strings attached that made business sustainability difficult, ironically.

When in receipt of Creative Scotland funding, you agree to pay all those involved in the project fair, living wages, as much as applicable. We already did this across our freelancers, so this was no concern. What *was* a concern was their reluctance to allow ourselves, the directors, to be remunerated fairly. The reluctance is understandable – why should the public purse pay a CEO their wage when their company should be the one to support that? If this was the case, Creative Scotland would no doubt be bombarded with a tsunami of applications from new CEOs suddenly very keen to be starting up their own company and looking for their first pay cheque before selling a single unit. We understand the rationale, but it created a challenge for us to identify how to pay ourselves when we're up £66,000 and have to operate as gainfully employed CEOs without the actual compensation. We were encouraged in application feedback to simply find a way to pay ourselves, without any actual guidance, so we did the only thing we could think of – get jobs elsewhere.

It is, anecdotally, something we often hear from other independent publishers across the UK. They are effectively working full-time jobs without security or financial support; it is often in the wee hours around "the real job" where they occur. There are bucks in the trend, such as publishers And Other Stories and Dead Ink, who are in receipt of regular funding from Arts Council England, and have the security to adapt, experiment and grow.

Returning to Jannat Ahmed's writing on Lucent Dreaming, she notes that they were similarly grateful for support from their own grant funder, the Books Council of Wales, though the funding for books "has not been properly adjusted to reflect the reality of our industry today."[56] They were encouraged to apply for part-time roles, despite the roadmap they laid out being based on two full-time members of staff; instead of accepting less just to have a seat at the table, they have instead chosen to not entirely close, but go slower and scale down. Ahmed's piece is another excellent read and captures what many publishers privately lament regarding manipulating their values to accommodate public funding structures:

> "I am not willing to sell my labour for less than I deserve, nor do I wish to set that precedent for others who are setting up or applying for funding, especially in the age of AI, when artists and creatives are already being exploited and devalued.

> "It wasn't about changing the culture in Wales, it was about changing the culture of publishing worldwide, one which felt wholly inaccessible. Later, when I set up our book publishing arm as a limited business, I knew why I wanted to publish the kind of work we do: because the work mattered. But Lucent has always been more than the people who started it. It's in all the people who believed in the dream and made it happen."[57]

As you can see, there were years in which we were able to pull income from 404 Ink to cover the most basic of hours, but at most we were receiving around £600 a month each for a little over a year. Other payments across the nine years were sporadic and modest, when the company cash flow could handle it. As we've allowed, it was a regular occurrence that when 404 Ink's cash position was healthy, our personal ones were not. When our personal finances were healthy, 404 Ink was neglected and the cash reserves fell, necessitating us to refocus our attentions to the company and invest more free labour. So, the tension kept returning and we realised that without consistent, predictable investment, it was impossible for 404 Ink *and* us to be financially sustained, it had to be either/or.

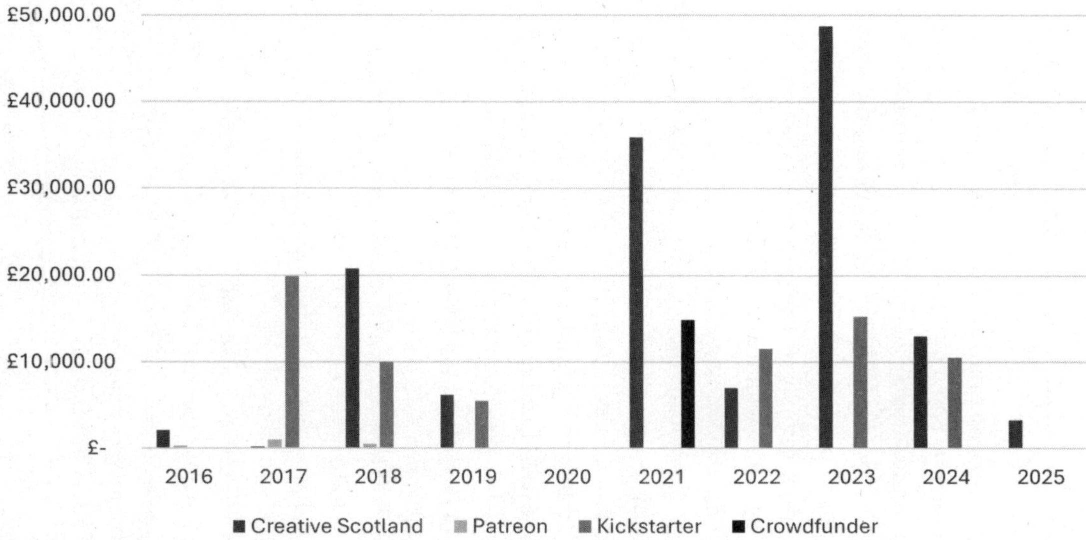

(This doesn't include one-off grants including £10,000 received from Scottish EDGE in 2018 and £3,017 from the Scottish Government in 2020 as part of the COVID hardship funds. Being one-off grant payments, we've left these out of analysis as they were specifically for business development and assistance respectively.)

To focus on 404 Ink's sustainability, we've collated the majority of external income we've received as part of specific fundraising campaigns or applications.

Altogether, we raised £89,500 via crowdfunding while receiving approximately £140,000 in Creative Scotland funding. It'd be disingenuous to categorise the crowdfunding income as generic funding, because we ran our crowdfunding campaigns as pre-order initiatives across anthologies, magazines and Inklings, so we classify that income as book sales, even though some generous customers did donate money with no order, or added extra money on top of their orders.

While crowdfunding was vital to our cash flow, the day-to-day book sales were the real income, of course. We've calculated that between October 2016 and August 2025, 404 Ink generated approximately £735,000 total revenue in book sales, breaking down as:

- £420,000 across 112,000 print units sold via the retail trade
- £110,000 across 13,500 print and ebook units sold via the 404 Ink website
- £90,000 via crowdfunding across approximately 6,600 print units and 1,600 ebook units
- £68,000 via Amazon across approximately 16,500 print units
- £18,700 via Amazon across 8,500 ebook units

- £3,000 via miscellaneous ebook retailers across 800 units
- And around £25,000 on trade sales made before we got distribution via BookSource in early 2017, so we lack the granular unit data from that period, unfortunately.

Based on these numbers and stretching clown math to its limit, we could clumsily claim that every £1 received from Creative Scotland was turned into £5.25 revenue. Or, every one of their pounds was turned into £2.14 for authors, editors, illustrators, assistants, interns, directors. Whatever way you want to slice that pie, we think we can confidently say that we used the public purse as well as we could have, investing as much as possible in the talent that carries the industry and contributing to its significant revenue.

We haven't even had space to discuss the £186,000 spent on book printing, the £40,000 paid to our sales teams in commission, the £30,000 spent on publicity campaigns, the accountants paid £27,000, the £18,000 paid in corporation tax and the £3,500 paid to interns, the finances in seeking international rights sales that could stretch the investment in titles further, showing our work has recompensed numerous people across myriad industries, not just our own.

We present these numbers not necessarily to gloat nor explain ourselves to the sceptics, but to exemplify that even the smallest of companies can punch far, far above their weight and truly contribute to a more equitable publishing culture, if determined enough.

However, yet again, these numbers don't provide the full fiscal picture. To complete our holistic analysis, we need to consider 404 Ink's yearly revenue and profit/loss reports. You can find reports of our basic finances on Companies House, but you won't see the narrative or the profit/loss. So here they are for your interest:

	Turnover	**Profit**
Y1 2016-2017:	£46,450	£15,193
Y2 2017-2018:	£77,320	£11,398
Y3 2018-2019:	£79,384	£8,745
Y4 2019-2020:	£43,019	£1,996
Y5 2020-2021:	£38,687	£31,074
Y6 2021-2022:	£59,009	-£14,001
Y7 2022-2023:	£99,791	£4,667
Y8 2023-2024:	£166,219	£1,098

Here we could talk about the predictable plummet in turnover during COVID-19, yet massive profit thanks to Creative Scotland funding landing in our bank account right before the end of our financial year, before we had a chance to spend any of it on what it was allocated for, totally skewing our accounts and creating a massive corporation tax bill. Or we could

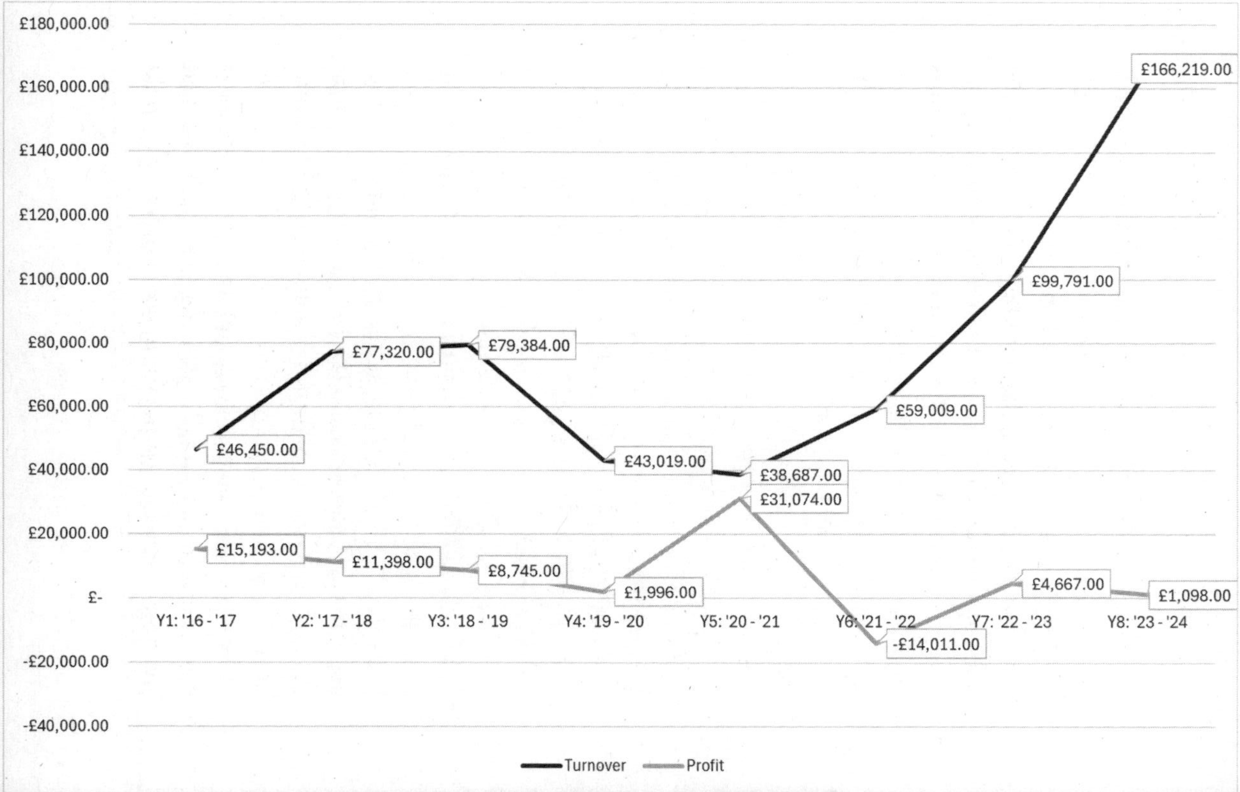
£180,000.00
£160,000.00
£140,000.00
£120,000.00
£100,000.00
£80,000.00
£60,000.00
£40,000.00
£20,000.00
£-
-£20,000.00
-£40,000.00
£46,450.00
£77,320.00
£79,384.00
£43,019.00
£38,687.00
£59,009.00
£99,791.00
£166,219.00
£15,193.00
£11,398.00
£8,745.00
£1,996.00
£31,074.00
-£14,011.00
£4,667.00
£1,098.00
Y1: '16 - '17
Y2: '17 - '18
Y3: '18 - '19
Y4: '19 - '20
Y5: '20 - '21
Y6: '21 - '22
Y7: '22 - '23
Y8: '23 - '24
Turnover
Profit

be stunned by the promising turnover trajectory from 2021 onwards against the languishing profit. However we want to interpret this, the holistic view is coming together, and it's saying that building business sustainability in publishing is slow and unpredictable. We know that publishers' backlists derive significant income in the long term and that in publishing, ten years still makes for a relatively youthful company,[58] so how long does it truly take to build said backlist? While our business plans looked three years in the future, which seemed like an eternity to us then, it might appear that for publishers to plan for their longevity, they need to be looking at *least* ten years into the future towards having that crucial backlist to rely on.

At 404 Ink, we can see that the Inklings titles we published in 2021 and 2022 are becoming our essential backlist titles keeping our turnover and cash flow afloat, and if we were to continue publishing past 2026, we now fully believe those would be the books keeping us in business so we could publish new frontlist titles and keep the cycle going. Sure, we would've had to increase the RRP and identify some new retailers, but they have the kind of brand recognition that we wanted 404 Ink to have in the early days.

We are reluctant to quote one of the world's more ruthless and unpleasant CEOs, but Amazon founder Jeff Bezos did say in 2011 that "if everything you do needs to work on a three-year time horizon, then you're competing against a lot of people… Just by lengthening the time horizon, you can engage in endeavours that you could never otherwise pursue."[59] It's hard to argue with the man who revolutionised book retail, whether you agree with his methods or not (we, unequivocably, do not), and we can unfortunately see in 404 Ink's operations that had we stuck it out and looked further into the future with our plans, we may have survived or even thrived, regardless of whether us founders had run out of steam to keep it going or not.

Crucially, to close 404 Ink with our turnover at its highest, and our reputation holding strong, is all we could have hoped for. To appropriate Kurt Cobain's infamous final words of "it's better to burn out than fade away", we want to wrap up the 404 Ink journey while offering this financial insight for anyone hoping to enter the industry as an entrepreneur, and retroactively performing a post-mortem to identify why the small publishing ecosystem collapsed under the pressures it couldn't overcome.

Predicting the future is a mug's game, but we can take a swing at identifying trends retroactively and a pattern seems to have emerged – the ten-year itch. The number of small to medium publishers that go on hiatus, pivot, consciously close, or collapse around the ten-year mark is notable.

There are statistical mantras regarding the failure rate of start-ups so repeatedly misquoted and unsourced they are practically meaningless, but some say most start-ups don't last five years and most of those that do are closed by ten, which seems to be an emerging pattern in publishing. However, from 2016 onwards, small publisher closures across the UK indicated that passing their tenth birthday is by no means a guarantee of security.

An inexhaustive sample of a baker's dozen of publishers shows that some don't or barely make it past five years, such as Fiction & Feeling, Cargo, Freight Books, Red Dog Press and Handheld Press, with Knights Of making eight years while some just about hold on until the ten-year period such as us, Unsung Stories, Leith Books, who appear to be in semi-hiatus, and Influx Press, who also went on hiatus around their tenth year before returning with more streamlined output and operations. BHP Comics closed around their twelfth year, and we've already discussed Unbound who just about made it to year fifteen, though we now know that operations appeared unstable many years prior to closure and natural selection probably should've seen them dissolved after ten years. Bucking the trend, Penned in the Margins went into indefinite hiatus in 2023 after almost twenty years, and Sandstone Press collapsed in their twenty-first year, seemingly unable to make the numbers work for the long term.

At the very least, around the ten-year point in publishing, for those still in operation, growth or pivoting appears essential to remain sustainable, whether that's changing outputs to be more in line with current market trends, or changing the leadership team – there are big decisions to be reckoned with to secure a future. If this cannot be done, it's unlikely the publisher will prevail, and this is a factor start-up publishers need to consider in their early years if they seek to be in the game for the long run. The moment for change will come; it's whether you are prepared for it, or caught off guard.

You might wonder why we seem to be quitting while we're ahead, and the truth is we don't feel ahead at all. In hindsight, we know that we should have been looking upwards of a decade forward in our business plan, but the idea of doing that now is exasperating. We can see the current literary ecosystem faltering for many and failing for some, as small publishers are undercapitalised and taken for granted by governments and funders. The era of relying on key social media platforms for book sales, as we did, has passed with little else replacing it. The pressure of unexpected and unpredictable additional admin and costs from the ongoing fallout of Brexit and a second Trump administration affects the smallest companies the most, constantly eating at razor-thin margins. We're seeing Silicon Valley-esque AI giants illegally devour thousands if not millions of books for their large language models, treating copyrighted work as fodder for their aspirational profits, authors and publishers be damned. We're at the mercy of these compounding pressures and see little way out without adopting huge changes that we genuinely don't want, or *can't* commit to as our priorities in life have moved away from 404 Ink.

Most small publishers are just one or two disastrous financial hits away from closure, due to, for example, unexpected stock returns from a major bookseller, or an industry shift where paper prices suddenly skyrocket and there's no way to mitigate. There are myriad ways publishers can end and it's often under the pressure of trying to exist indefinitely. We're quitting while we're ahead because we recognise we *don't* have to exist indefinitely and we're comfortable in knowing we made our waves for a decade before bowing out. Not everyone gets an ending on their own terms, and we wanted to be one of the few who was able to write their own.

If you are hoping to start your own publishing company, we can only say "do it", but please do it with your eyes open, looking to the long-term future, because you may end up in it longer than you ever anticipated, as we did. What might seem like an innovative, zeitgeist idea right now just might be, but it might be the catalyst for so much more, towards a wild and varied career in the arts with twists and turns you'd never dream possible. We have both worked with incredible collaborators and projects, and it was largely thanks to our work as 404 Ink putting us on people's radars, giving us a sense of legitimacy. Even if we couldn't quite make 404 Ink the sustainable business we aspired it to be, we still reap the benefits professionally and we hope to never take that for granted. Nor will we take for granted being able to be a first step on many authors' journeys; to see their books reach readers, and careers grow from here is something we will always be incredibly proud of.

It is a privilege to be a publisher and make a living from it, even modestly, to pay this forward, share our insights; and while we look back and can unpick what we wish we'd known, or what we'd do differently, we know that we did our best at the time and made our mark. We couldn't possibly ask for any more than that.

Conclusion

It is odd to effectively write your own company's eulogy, especially while it's not quite dead yet. Much of the journey documented has been rocky. You might have wondered if we even like publishing or when we were going to be done moaning about it. For reassurance, yes, we promise we did enjoy publishing (and do still) and we're almost finished moaning, don't worry. We are done with 404 Ink, but not with publishing itself.

During one of our annual meetings where we took stock of 404 Ink's operations strategically, we looked to our original business plan with the bullet points compared against these latest activities and how they matched with our professional aims. Nearly ten years on, our attempt to update our mission statement and vision with new aims fell flat. After hours spent sitting at our dining tables, the same labrador nudging for attention, we found ourselves circling the same issue we had discussed for years by this point: a realistic, sustainable business plan requires 404 Ink to grow financially, or at the very least keep up with rates of inflation. Staying the same modest size that we want to remain at requires us to, ironically, grow. To stay the same, we need to publish even more now that any profit from sales goes less distance, and we recently reported an overall loss in our annual accounts! If we could responsibly publish more, we would have done that already. Do we have it in us – now in our mid-30s, with other demanding jobs that actually pay us alongside this labour of love, and families to be responsible for – to start this mission statement anew and pursue this necessary growth?

We didn't, and the reason was simple. Growth cannot be the sole purpose for 404 Ink's operations. That is not what drives us. It is the concept that has, in fact, plagued us over the years, clouding our vision, leading us to emulate what the bigger publishers do with far less capital, chase investment, break our company down into pounds and pennies to woo some angel investor who just does not exist for us. We were going around in circles trying to conceive how now, at ten years deep, we would suddenly crack this issue and achieve that elusive "security" and "stability" on the other side of the DIY, scrappy upstarts we were.

In taking stock of 404 Ink's impact over the last years, considering the cost of the passion we self-exploited and how far we had managed to professionalise within and outwith our various mantras, realising that to push forward with the company's operations as-is is to plateau, to potentially be diminished by our own lack of motivation to chase goals that do not really drive us, the conversation turned in a different direction:

"Are we happy with what 404 Ink has achieved?"

"Yes."

"Do we think we can make a demonstrably bigger positive impact for another ten years?"

"No."

"Do we have any meaningful way to make 404 Ink financially supportive of not just our authors and contractors, but us too?"

"No."

"Do we still believe in our makeshift slogan of 'publishing loudly'?"

"Yes."

"Are we the right people to do this any longer, given where we are in life?"

"No."

"Should we close the company on its tenth anniversary?"

"Yes."

"Are we breaking up?!"

"Oh, god..."

Suddenly, excitement replaced trepidation. What had been an entire day of staring at the same blank business plan and going in circles immediately began to fizz to life: we could make a blueprint on how to (hopefully) ethically close a publisher; we could explore an author-first wind down of the company; we could use the time to talk to other publishers; we could approach industry press to highlight why ethics and process matters as much in the end as it does in the beginning. We could pay it forward in our last year by sharing more information than ever before. We could run initiatives to raise money in support of fellow or aspiring small, independent publishers who are driven by ethos but trapped in the maw of capitalism and funding uncertainty. We could write a book (hello) on what it meant to run 404 Ink, to give people insight into the process, to further demystify a continually opaque industry. We could throw one hell of a funeral to send us off. It may not be as inspirational as pushing forward for another ten years, supporting more authors and collaborators, getting a *Sunday Times* bestseller or Booker win, or nailing this whole publishing thing, but what if we could close as we launched: loudly, and with intention.

When we announced in July 2025 that we were going to close 404 Ink a year later, we were met with public and private mourning, but to us, it is not something to mourn. It was certainly nice to receive a Lifetime

Achievement Award from *The Skinny*'s Besties at the Edinburgh Festivals to mark our closure, and it has humbly skewed some of our more cynical perceptions of our work, but we are one small stitch in a tapestry of those carving out their spaces in culture.

We have spent the subsequent months in collaboration with Sara Hunt at Saraband, with whom many of our Inklings series and select titles will continue to be published. We've been meeting with publishers interested in taking forward other 404 Ink authors, writing this book, speaking to other publishers struggling with their own journey, working out how to bring a fundraiser for these publishers to fruition upon our closure, and we have been looking to the future, collectively and individually.

So, what would it take to be a publisher today, if we were to try this again?

Open eyes, for one. An adaptability to the shifting, scattered and particularly toxic strands of social media and routes to audiences. A dose of reality that publishing can be great and it can be hard; it is often both.

The team around you makes or breaks it. For us, the duology of approach and experience found a balance that worked for us. We couldn't do it solo. We take our hats off to those who do. We scrambled to get the best sales team for us because, my god, when you find the ones who get it, the difference is astronomical (hi, Inpress, shout out to you).

A mission is vital to stand apart. We see it in our favourite Scottish bookshops – the radical Lighthouse, the queer Category Is, the community-serving Portobello Bookshop and Argonaut. In publishing, Magic Cat, one-time fellow shortlistees for Small Press of the Year at the British Book Awards, not only swept the award, but by the next award cycle had outgrown it entirely, surpassing the £5 million turnover threshold. Since the press founded after they became mothers, we have the additional admiration of a publisher finding balance in areas we never could. No matter the heights they reach, "the goal is to stay fiercely independent," said co-founder Rachel Williams, "and, over the next five years, be the leading children's specialists in the UK and the house that any author who wants to make a children's book should come to."[60] To see genuine success in contemporary independent publishing is something we hope continues.

Of course, to be as canny as Magic Cat with the cash, you need to be financially literate above all else. We can't in good conscience offer entrepreneurial advice without insisting that a budding publisher *needs* a good accountant and basic financial understanding. We blustered in with neither and learned on the go but luckily find the finances quite fascinating along with endlessly frustrating, so we actually enjoy working on the annual accounts and budgeting for the future. Be familiar with

P&Ls, balance sheets, cash flow, projections, tax procedures and funding avenues. This knowledge gives you power and control over your own operations in an industry certain to challenge that. Far from the romantic visions that often drive us to publishing, the industry will always be a business first and foremost, and you have to treat it as such.

There has been a notion, too, post-Unbound, that crowdfunding isn't the viable financial buoy publishing hoped it to be. The fact is, it *is*, when done *properly*. Dead Ink is one of the only independent presses we have seen crack a Patreon system, with 404 monthly backers (nice) as we write. We see Kickstarter continuing to bolster projects big and small, too, and these routes exist for those bold enough to carve their space there. We see arts grant bodies partnering and experimenting more with crowdfunding support. It's challenging, but the payoffs can be invaluable.

It is time-consuming to foster a community, but all the more rewarding and supportive to be part of one. The social media communities we launched in no longer exist; the gatekeepers at the top are no longer the tastemakers they were. Publishers continue to operate opaquely behind the scenes, and sites like TikTok are forcing them – even the Big Five – to put their faces in front of the camera and create new strands to their branding, changing how they interact with readers.

Such digital presences are not for everyone, and they can be draining to maintain consistently (which is crucial for the ever-influential "algorithm"), so finding your community and building methods to reach readers in a way that is natural to you is key.

Substack also has potential for publishers – moving on from pithy 140-character posts of ye olde Twitter days to longer-form content. Gone are the goals to be reviewed or even advertised in *The Guardian* or *Bustle*, which was once a "made it" moment. Now, we would seek for our books to be included in Substacks such as *shit you should care about* by Lucy Blakiston, which does what it says on the tin with wit and personality,[61] or on *Service95*, where popstar Dua Lipa puts carefully selected books in front of a new readership who are there for her stamp of approval. The tastemakers are more democratised and far from the traditional broadsheet platforms that publishers coveted. Substack also hosts *Extra Teeth* literary magazine's online publication *With Bite*, which extends their brand beyond the printed page, and Sam Jordison's *Pressing issues*, which discusses the latest issues of publishing through the perspective of his own Galley Beggar Press.[62]

Being environmentally conscious is pertinent, too. We reckoned with this a lot over our time – using only FSC-certified paper, the most eco-friendly packaging we could afford, and cover production considerations. We've looked at lower-carbon travel options and carbon offsetting by planting trees over the years. A lot of small presses bake this into their approaches and some have donated a percentage of sales towards local trusts to plant trees in Welsh woodland areas,[63] where the Northern Fiction Alliance ran The Green Book Fair, an online forum designed for the environmentally conscious global publishing community.[64] This seems to be one area taken more seriously at a higher level, too: Macmillan aims "to do less harm and more good to the Earth",[65] while Penguin Random House has set a target of net neutrality by 2030.[66] Many publishers and similar stakeholders have signed the Publishers Association's "Publishing Declares" climate action plan.[67]

Fly on the Wall Press, founded by Isabelle Kenyon in 2018, have also launched their Publishing Academy, turning their attention behind the scenes with a brilliant initiative to demystify the industry for aspiring publishers. It is something akin to what we had hoped to achieve with our own Publishing 101 newsletter of advice for aspiring publishers that never got off the ground due to other commitments. We need people to keep pushing for such new ideas that can open doors for others – some will fail, like our own, but others will soar, and it is the consistent push towards transparency that can hopefully make this the norm.

Initiatives like these are vital for the route into and through the publishing experience, to mould your own way. We say this as two people who did complete their

Masters in Publishing Studies, but degrees are only one avenue to this industry. We attribute our years spent in fandoms and music journalism as equally if not more valuable in some elements of what we sought to do.

There is a power in numbers, in community and connecting together – the aforementioned open letter from independent publishers called attention to the concerns of publishing from a range of small dynamic presses, noting, "If we do not enact change now, there is a real possibility that many indie presses will be unable to continue operating in the next five years, indefinitely altering the breadth and diversity of the UK's literary landscape."[68] There was a crucial misassumption in a response from the Independent Publishers Guild – "to be independent is not to be small and struggling, but to have huge potential for growth",[69] with recommendations of their own upskilling and resources towards preparing for tough business environments. We do all know we don't have to be small and struggling – just not all of us want to grow into a Faber, or a Nosy Crow. They are instrumental to the industry, yes; small presses are, too. We have been upskilling and sharing resources for years, *decades*, already. Some of us want to sustain smaller operational levels, to merely know we will survive as we seek to create and foster cultural value without the stress of our lives and livelihood hanging in the balance of "growth potential" to do so.

We come back, often, to the notion that the small can be impactful when focused and collated. We see the Northern Fiction Alliance, the radical publishing collective in the North of England; Small Press Scotland CIC, the new non-profit dedicated to uplifting the small press scene in all its forms; the Scottish BPOC Writers Network, who provide advocacy, literary events and professional development opportunities for Black writers and writers of colour; Fossil Free Books, who have seismically and materially made shifts via their advocacy in their first years alone; Publishers for Palestine, the global collective who stand for justice, freedom of expression and the power of the written word.

Away from the collective and on our own, we cannot claim that we did everything in 404 Ink perfectly, nor do we have a solution to many of its woes. We don't even claim, truly, that our story is one worth reading; we are just another company that ultimately came and went in a climate that makes survival increasingly difficult. What we do stand firm on, and always will, is that it was never possible alone.

Over the handful of months we wrote this book, we witnessed a wave of publishers we admire close, unable to find a sustainable way forward, with even more privately admitting to us that they would soon follow suit. They cited the same things, time and again, the pressures that grind down so many in the arts. There is a shifting tide, from the inside at least, towards a worrying tipping point. We suppose that is why thc story of 404 Ink is one we wanted to tell as we hear the private conversations, knowing it is time to share these issues more publicly as our decade in this arena comes to its own conclusion.

Time is running out for the cultural infrastructure that only works for high-growth-potential companies, or rich tech bros blustering in with AI to revolutionise an industry by plagiarising its artistic and creative heart, as we're seeing today. To us, a reflective and inclusive environment is not just for the benefit of reading culture: there needs to be space to create, experiment, fail, find new ways in, bring others up, have relative financial security, create platforms that break apart from the larger monopolies. Some of the most groundbreaking and vital publishing is happening in the margins, where the struggles are the most potent. We cannot afford to lose that.

References

1 "Artists demand National Endowment for the Arts roll back Trump restrictions." Adrian Horton, *The Guardian*, 19 February 2025. theguardian.com/culture/2025/feb/19/national-endowment-arts-dei-trump. Accessed 17 January 2026.

2 "The UK Publishing Industry in 2025" *George Walkley/ Outside Context*. georgewalkley.com/UK-Publishing-Industry-2025/. Accessed 17 January 2026.

3 "Authors await overdue payments as publisher Unbound goes into administration." Lucy Knight, *The Guardian*, 18 March 2025. theguardian.com/books/2025/mar/18/authors-await-overdue-payments-as-publisher-unbound-goes-into-administration. Accessed 17 January 2026.

4 "UK publishing revenue exceeds £7 billion for first time." *Publishers Association*, 7 May 2024. publishers.org.uk/publishingin2023/. Accessed 17 January 2026.

5 "The Writers' Conference 2025 – Keynote Speakers & Partial Programme Announced." *Arts Derbyshire*, 21 February 2025. artsderbyshire.org.uk/news/jobs-training-commissions-opportunities/the-writers-conference-2025-keynote-speakers-partial-programme-announced/. Accessed 17 January 2026.

6 "Where Your Passion Meets the Market." Rachelle Gardner, 8 October 2019. rachellegardner.com/passion-meets-market/. Accessed 17 January 2026.

7 "How to get into publishing." Daniel Higginbotham, *Prospects,* February 2025. prospects.ac.uk/jobs-and-work-experience/job-sectors/media-and-internet/how-to-get-into-publishing. Accessed 17 January 2026.

8 "Brand New Mindless Self Indulgence Record!" kickstarter.com/projects/1268472090/brand-new-mindless-self-indulgence-record. Accessed 17 January 2026.

9 "TLC is BACK to make our FINAL ALBUM with YOU!" kickstarter.com/projects/1507621537/tlc-is-back-to-make-our-final-album-with-you/. Accessed 17 January 2026.

10 "Theatre Is Evil: the album, art book and tour." kickstarter.com/projects/amandapalmer/amanda-palmer-the-new-record-art-book-and-tour. Accessed 17 January 2026.

11 "The 'nasty women' shaking up the book industry." Kirstyn Smith, *Huck*, 12 March 2017. huckmag.com/article/404-ink-nasty-women-trump-publishing-books. Accessed 17 January 2026.

12 "The Good Immigrant review – an unflinching dialogue about race and racism in the UK." Sandeep Parmar, *The Guardian*, 22 September 2016. theguardian.com/books/2016/sep/22/good-immigrant-review-nikesh-shukla-britain-racist. Accessed 17 January 2026.

13 "Scottish indie looks to kick up an Ink with launch collection." Sarah Shaffi, *The Bookseller*, 5 December 2016. thebookseller.com/news/scottish-indie-looks-kick-ink-launch-collection-441231. Accessed 17 January 2026.

14 "Books To Read If You're An Activist." Sharmaine Lovegrove, *Elle*, 8 March 2017. elle.com/uk/life-and-culture/culture/articles/a34473/books-to-read-as-an-activist/. Accessed 17 January 2026.

15 "TikTok Users, Stats, Data & Trends for 2025." *DataReportal*, 12 March 2025. datareportal.com/essential-tiktok-stats. Accessed 17 January 2026.

16 “X Users, Stats, Data & Trends for 2025.” *DataReportal*, 12 March 2025. datareportal.com/essential-x-stats. Accessed 17 January 2026.

17 “OWN IT! founders reflect on first 10 years of the company as they plot next decade.” Philip Jones, *The Bookseller*, 2 September 2025. thebookseller.com/news/own-it-founders-reflect-on-first-10-years-of-the-company-as-they-plot-next-decade. Accessed 17 January 2026.

18 “Survival is the focus, says Knights Of co-founder.” Ruth Comerford, *The Bookseller*, 13 May 2020. thebookseller.com/news/survival-focus-says-knights-co-founder-1203366. Accessed 17 January 2026.

19 “CRISIS FUNDING FOR INCLUSIVE PUBLISHERS.” crowdfunder.co.uk/p/inclusive-indies. Accessed 17 January 2026.

20 “‘Sexists need not apply’: publisher refuses to look at manuscripts addressed to ‘Dear sirs’.” Alison Flood, *The Guardian*, 28 September 2017. theguardian.com/books/2017/sep/28/sexists-need-not-apply-publisher-refuses-to-look-at-manuscripts-addressed-to-dear-sirs. Accessed 17 January 2026.

21 “‘UK publishing benefits a lot from Irish cultural output!’ Irish Publishing At Large — In Conversation with Tramp Press.” *Turnaround*, 29 March 2023. theturnaroundblog.com/2023/03/29/uk-publishing-benefits-a-lot-from-irish-cultural-output-irish-publishing-at-large-in-conversation-with-tramp-press/. Accessed 17 January 2026.

22 “Who gets to be a ‘Scottish writer’?” *Extra Teeth Magazine*, 24 September 2025. extrateethmagazine.substack.com/p/who-gets-to-be-a-scottish-writer. Accessed 17 January 2026.

23 “Indie Hajar Press launches ‘to tackle racism in publishing’.” Ruth Comerford, *The Bookseller*, 10 August 2020. the-

bookseller.com/news/new-political-press-launches-1214234. Accessed 17 January 2026.

24 thegoodliteraryagency.org/. Accessed 17 January 2026.

25 "'The gesture speaks for itself': Germans respond to Musk's apparent Nazi salute." Kate Connolly, *The Guardian*, 21 January 2025. theguardian.com/technology/2025/jan/21/the-gesture-speaks-for-itself-germans-divided-over-musks-apparent-nazi-salute. Accessed 17 January 2026.

26 "Inside Elon Musk's Intense Daily Routine." *CEO Today*, 14 February 2025. ceotodaymagazine.com/2025/02/inside-elon-musks-intense-daily-routine/. Accessed 17 January 2026.

27 "The morning routines of CEOs and founders, from Airbnb's Brian Chesky to Melinda French Gates." Jaures Yip, Jordan Hart and Lakshmi Varanasi, *Business Insider*, 24 June 2025. businessinsider.com/ceo-morning-routines. Accessed 17 January 2026.

28 "Molly Mae: How She Became Creative Director Of PLT At 22 | 110" The Diary of a CEO, *YouTube*, 13 December 2021. youtube.com/watch?v=6WgIOKFLrHY. Accessed 17 January 2026.

29 "Kim Kardasian's Business Advice for Women in Business." Variety, *YouTube*, 14 October 2022. youtube.com/shorts/Daq55GVdGJc. Accessed 17 January 2026.

30 "We are tired af." *404 Ink*, 21 December 2017. 404ink.com/blog/2017/12/21/we-are-tired-af. Accessed 17 January 2026.

31 "Thoughts on… Lucent Dreaming [by Jannat Ahmed]." Jannat Ahmed, *Lucent Dreaming*. lucentdreaming.com/thoughts-on-lucent-dreaming-by-jannat-ahmed/. Accessed 17 January 2026.

32 "Boldwood Books looks to future growth after success at last year's Nibbies." Philip Jones, *The Bookseller*, 7 May 2024. thebookseller.com/trade-interviews/boldwood-books-looks-to-future-growth-after-success-at-last-years-nibbies. Accessed 17 January 2026.

33 "Throw the book at publishing internships." Suzanne Collier, *The Guardian*, 23 March 2010. theguardian.com/careers/careers-blog/publishing-internships-suzanne-collier. Accessed 17 January 2026.

34 "Unpaid internships 'should be banned to build diversity in publishing'." Alison Flood, *The Guardian*, 9 July 2015. theguardian.com/books/2015/jul/09/unpaid-internships-should-be-banned-to-build-diversity-in-publishing. Accessed 17 January 2026.

35 "Unpaid internships 'locking out' young working-class people from careers." Richard Adams, *The Guardian*, 23 January 2025. theguardian.com/society/2025/jan/23/unpaid-internships-young-working-class-people-careers. Accessed 17 January 2026.

36 "'Let them read books': why publishing needs to pay its interns." Mat Toor, *The Bookseller*, 4 May 2016. thebookseller.com/comment/let-them-read-books-why-publishing-needs-pay-its-interns-328110. Accessed 17 January 2026.

37 "'Morally wrong' unpaid internships earn trade 'poor reputation'." Natasha Onwuemezi, *The Bookseller*, 1 August 2017. thebookseller.com/news/unpaid-internships-ruining-industry-reputation-595566. Accessed 17 January 2026.

38 "PRH UK to pay work experience participants in diversity drive." Katherine Cowdrey, *The Bookseller*, 18 April 2017. thebookseller.com/news/prh-uk-pay-work-experience-diversity-drive-536536. Accessed 17 January 2026.

39 "A profession struggling to sustain itself." Martin Reed, *The Society of Authors*, 6 December 2022. societyofauthors.org/2022/12/06/a-profession-struggling-to-sustain-itself/. Accessed 17 January 2026.

40 "The 15 Highest-Paid Authors of All Time." Sarah Rexford, *Self Publishing*, 10 December 2023. selfpublishing.com/highest-paid-authors/. Accessed 17 January 2026.

41 "How do authors get paid?" *The Society of Authors*. societyofauthors.org/where-we-stand/special-sales/how-do-authors-get-paid/. Accessed 17 January 2026.

42 "The Big Five Publishers Statistics." Dimitrije Curcic, *WordsRated*, 17 November 2022. wordsrated.com/the-big-five-publishers-statistics/. Accessed 17 January 2026.

43 "Patchy and Negligible." Claire Squires, *Bella Caledonia*, 4 June 2019. bellacaledonia.org.uk/2019/06/04/patchy-and-negligible/. Accessed 17 January 2026.

44 "Burchill cancels new contract after publisher linked to far right group." Mark Chandler, *The Bookseller*, 16 March 2021. thebookseller.com/news/burchill-cancels-contract-after-publisher-linked-white-nationalists-1249109. Accessed 17 January 2026.

45 "Chitra Ramaswamy – On A Lifetime of Ticking Boxes." Chitra Ramaswamy, *Literature Alliance Scotland*. literaturealliancescotland.co.uk/contact-us/chitra-ramaswamy-on-a-lifetime-of-ticking-boxes/. Accessed 17 January 2026.

46 Saha, A., & van Lente, S. (2022). "Diversity, media and racial capitalism: a case study on publishing". *Ethnic and Racial Studies*, *45*(16), 216–236. doi.org/10.1080/01419870.2022.2032250.

47 "State of play: can stalled momentum in Black publishing be undone?" Natasha Onwuemezi, *The Bookseller*, 28 June

2025. thebookseller.com/trade-interviews/state-of-play-can-stalled-momentum-in-black-publishing-be-undone. Accessed 17 January 2026.

48 "The Quine Report." quinereport.com. Accessed 17 January 2026.

49 Throsby, D. (2017). "Commerce or culture? Australian book industry policy in the twenty-first century". In A. Mannion, M. Weber, & K. Day (Eds.), *Publishing means business: Australian perspectives* (pp. 1-21). Monash University Publishing.

50 "What does it cost to produce a book?" Sam Jordison, Galley Beggar - Pressing issues, *Substack*, 25 September 2025. samj.substack.com/p/what-does-it-cost-to-produce-a-book. Accessed 17 January 2026.

51 Bhaskar, Michael. *The Content Machine: Towards a Theory of Publishing from the Printing Press to the Digital Network*, Anthem Press, 2013. *ProQuest Ebook Central*, ebookcentral.proquest.com/lib/stir/detail.action?docID=1212741.

52 "Open letter on the future of small press publishing in the UK." *The Bookseller*, 10 October 2025. thebookseller.com/comment/open-letter-on-the-future-of-small-press-publishing-in-the-uk. Accessed 17 January 2026.

53 "Profile reports second-best year ever but turnover down on 2023-24 peak." Lauren Brown, *The Bookseller*, 31 October 2025. thebookseller.com/news/profile-reports-second-best-year-ever-but-turnover-down-on-2023-24-peak. Accessed 17 January 2026.

54 "Bloomsbury reports £24m profit for first six months of 2025." Maia Snow, *The Bookseller*, 23 October 2025. thebookseller.com/news/bloomsbury-reports-24m-profit-for-first-six-months-of-2025. Accessed 17 January 2026.

55 "Canongate reports turnover of £17.9m as authors and agents paid £8.8m." Melina Spanoudi, *The Bookseller*, 8 November 2024. thebookseller.com/news/canongate-reports-turnover-of-179m-as-authors-and-agents-paid-88m. Accessed 17 January 2026.

56 "Thoughts on… the Future of Publishing [by Jannat Ahmed]." Jannat Ahmen, *Lucent Dreaming*. lucentdreaming.com/thoughts-on-the-future-of-publishing-by-jannat-ahmed/. Accessed 17 January 2026.

57 Ibid.

58 Squires, C., Markou, H. "An Ecosystem Model of Small and Medium Sized Enterprises Publisher 'Tiers': Publisher Size, Sustainability and Cultural Policy". *Pub Res Q* 37, 420–438 (2021). doi.org/10.1007/s12109-021-09811-y

59 "Jeff Bezos's 10,000 Year Clock and Thinking Long Term." Dmitry Dragilev, *Zurb*, 17 November 2011. zurb.com/blog/jeff-bezos-s-10-000-year-clock-and-thinki. Accessed 17 January 2026.

60 "Proudly independent: Magic Cat Publishing plans for the future." Caroline Carpenter, *The Bookseller*, 11 March 2025. thebookseller.com/features/proudly-independent-magic-cat-publishing-plans-for-the-future. Accessed 17 January 2026.

61 "shit you should care about." *Substack*. shityoushouldcareabout.substack.com. Accessed 17 January 2026.

62 "Galley Beggar - Pressing issues." *Substack*. samj.substack.com. Accessed 17 January 2026.

63 "New indie publisher to use books sales to help restore a Welsh woodland." *Nation Cymru*, 18 July 2021. nation.cymru/culture/new-indie-publisher-to-use-books-sales-to-help-restore-a-welsh-woodland/. Accessed 17 January 2026.

64 "Northern Fiction Alliance announces return of The Green Book Fair for second year." Lauren Brown, *The Bookseller*, 16 October 2024. thebookseller.com/news/northern-fiction-alliance-announces-return-of-the-green-book-fair-for-second-year. Accessed 17 January 2026.

65 "Macmillan Sustainability." sustainability.macmillan.com. Accessed 17 January 2026.

66 "Environment & Sustainability." social-impact.penguinrandomhouse.com/our-commitments/enviro-ment-sustainability/. Accessed 17 January 2026.

67 "Publishing Declares Climate Action." publishingdeclares.com/home. Accessed 17 January 2026.

68 "Open letter on the future of small press publishing in the UK." *The Bookseller*, 10 October 2025. thebookseller.com/comment/open-letter-on-the-future-of-small-press-publishing-in-the-uk. Accessed 17 January 2026.

69 "The rollercoaster ride of independence." Bridget Shine, *The Bookseller*, 14 October 2025. thebookseller.com/comment/the-rollercoaster-ride-of-independence. Accessed 17 January 2026.

Acknowledgements

They say that to raise a child takes a village, so to run a publishing company takes its own expansive community. A city, even. While we can't name every member of our community that helped us, bolstered us, consoled and supported us over the past ten years, we do not take for granted every kindness and the generosity shown from them.

To the authors who trusted us with their words and their work, it was not possible without you. To those who met with us, mentored us across the way, distributors, sales team, every kind word, every shared resource, everyone who held part of 404 up to allow us to reach ten years, we thank you.

404 Ink started as an offhand idea we wanted to give a try. Ten years on, our lives have changed immeasurably. To you, who reads this, or has ever read a 404 book: thank you.

Heather's acknowledgements

The biggest thanks to Callum for not only being down for me randomly deciding to launch a company when we were both very young and very skint, but for being unquestionably supportive and understanding when 404 was all-consuming at its highs, and its not-so-highs. I couldn't have survived this without you.

My two girls who have no real idea what I do right now, but seem jazzed about it because it involves making books. Nothing else compares to you, really.

Luna, the canine mascot who was there at inception and is still there at the end, mooching snacks and gate-crashing interviews.

To my mum and dad who similarly were down, and endlessly supportive, of this career path, even if you've attended some events or read some books you wouldn't have otherwise. I've felt that no matter the job I chose, I'd have your full backing to find my way. Also, to my Uncle George, no longer here, who tracked our newspaper clippings and told me of the story he wanted to go on to write, and said he'd love to see me write a book one day. Maybe not the one you envisaged, but we'll take it, I hope.

To my ride-or-dies Claire, Charley and Becky, you have held my sanity since our teens even though we are many miles apart most days, and Kirstyn who may be travelling the world but is never able to escape me for consistently buoying me whenever I'm in doubt. To all who have given me time, advice and mentorship, of which there is an endless list, I am grateful, always.

It is a genuine rarity to click so swiftly with someone professionally and this is not a journey that would have been possible, or indeed as survivable, without Laura, the more reasoned balance to my sky-high ideas. There is also nothing I can be more grateful for than you keeping the 404 ship sailing so I could have the space to be a mum, and that is a gift that I can never really repay.

I do not like to be perceived – especially being sentimental – but here we are. Love you all.

Laura's acknowledgements

Firstly, thanks to Emma Barnes for the unfiltered professional and life advice that has led me to consider you my unofficial mentor in life, whether you know it or not. You gave me some vital perspective when I needed it the most, and I possibly wouldn't be where I am professionally without that.

To my bridesmaids (when you're bridesmaids once, you're bridesmaids forever, right?) Róisín and Aija, you've individually listened to my endlessly conflicted feelings about this profession of mine, and my personal endeavours along the way, with grace and generosity. Even when we're too busy or too geographically separated to catch up, I know we've got each other's backs. Thank you for all your wisdom and commiseration over the years.

Heather, our yin and yang brought us this far and while I know we're happy to move on from 404, I'm still sad to lose our effortless dynamic and seamless workflow. Our partnership showed me my potential in a way that doing this on my own could never do. Thank you for the journey.

I must thank those who were there at the beginning of 404 Ink's journey and are no longer here: thanks Grandad, Gran and Dad. I don't think you quite understood why I wanted to run a company without being paid but you supported me nonetheless. Hope I did you all proud in some way.

Mum, you've bought every single 404 Ink book and listened to all my borderline libellous moaning over the years, a lot of which you'll find familiar in this book, albeit toned down. You've been endlessly supportive regardless of the ideas being good or not, and I'm so thankful for all you've done for me across my thirty-five years. Love you.

Errol, we started dating the week *Nasty Women* came out and you were so patient when 404 Ink took everything I had, leaving little for you. Not much seems to have changed as I write these acknowledgements with my noise-cancelling headphones on, having ignored you all day to get this bloody book finished. You're endlessly understanding, supportive, caring, insightful and, most importantly, you make me laugh when just about nothing else can. You know me better than I know myself and I love being your wife. I love you, so much.

404 Ink Bibliography

2016

404 Ink, Literary Magazine #1: Error

2017

Nasty Women
Hings by Chris McQueer
404 Ink, Literary Magazine #2: F-Word
The Last Days of James Scythe by Creeper (under the pseudonym Lilly Banning)
404 Ink, Literary Magazine #3: Power

2018

On the Edges of Vision by Helen McClory
Mayhem & Death by Helen McClory
We Shall Fight Until We Win, edited by Nyla Ahmad and Sha Nazir. Co-published with BHP Comics.
404 Ink, Literary Magazine #4: Ink
The Goldblum Variations by Helen McClory
For Every One by Jason Reynolds. Co-published with Knights Of.

2019

We Were Always Here: A Queer Words Anthology, edited by Ryan Vance and Michael Lee Richardson
Let Me Tell You This by Nadine Aisha Jassat

Animals Eat Each Other by Elle Nash
404 Ink, Literary Magazine #5: Space
Constitution Street by Jemma Neville
Never, Ever Take Anybody's Advice on Anything by Euan Lownie
404 Ink, Literary Magazine #6: Earth

2020

Checkpoint: How Video Games Power Up Minds, Kick Ass and Save Lives by Joe Donnelly

2021

Love That Journey for Me: The Queer Revolution of Schitt's Creek by Emily Garside
On His Royal Badness: The Life and Legacy of Prince's Fashion by Casci Ritchie
The Appendix: Transmasculine Joy in a Transphobic Culture by Liam Konemann
The New University: Local Solutions to a Global Crisis by James Coe
The End: Surviving the World Through Imagined Disasters by Katie Goh
Flip the Script: How Women Came to Rule Hip Hop by Arusa Qureshi
Blind Spot: Exploring and Educating on Blindness by Maud Rowell
No Man's Land: Living Between Two Cultures by Anne East

2022

At Least This I Know by Andrés N. Ordorica
The Arena of the Unwell by Liam Konemann
Nudes by Elle Nash
They Came to Slay: The Queer Culture of D&D by Thom James Carter

Whatever Next?: On Adult Adoptee Identities by Josphine Jay, Adaline Bara, and Hannah Feben-Smith
Sons and Others: On Loving Male Survivors by Tanaka Mhishi
No Dice: Gambling and Risk in Modern Culture by Nathan Charles
New Skin for the Old Ceremony: A Kirtan by Arun Sood
Now Go: On Grief and Studio Ghibli by Karl Thomas Smith
The Loki Variations: The Man, The Myth, The Mischief by Karl Johnson
Carrie Kills A Man: A Memoir by Carrie Marshall

2023

Hair/Power: Essays on Control and Freedom by Kajal Odedra
BFFs: The Radical Potential of Female Friendship by Anahit Behrooz
We're Falling Through Space: Doctor Who and Celebrating the Mundane by J. David Reed
Deeping It: Colonialism, Culture and Criminalisation of UK Drill by Adèle Oliver
Machine Readable Me: The Hidden Ways Tech Shapes our Identities by Zara Rahman
The Last Day Before Exile: Stories of Resistance, Displacement and Finding Home by Selin Bucak

2024

All the Violet Tiaras: Queering the Greek Myths by Jean Menzies
Gathering: Women of Colour on Nature, edited by Durre Shahwar and Nasia Sarwar-Skuse
Fragile Animals by Genevieve Jagger
Electric Dreams: On Sex Robots and Failed Promises of Capitalism by Heather Parry
Happy Death Club: Essays on Death, Grief and Bereavement Across Cultures by Naomi Westerman

Victor & Barry's Kelvinside Compendium: A Meander Down Memory Close by Alan Cumming and Forbes Masson
Blitzkrieg Bops: A Brief History of Punks at War by Alli Patton
Solemates: A History of our Fetish for Feet by Adam Zmith

2025

Fierce Salvage: A Queer Words Anthology, edited by Ryan Vance and Michael Lee Richardson
Look, Don't Touch: Reflections on the Freedom to Feel by layla-roxanne hill and Francesca Sobande
Revolutionary Desires: The Political Power of the Sex Scene by Xuanlin Tham
Roses for Hedone: On Queer Hedonism and World-Making Through Pleasure by Prishita Maheshwari-Aplin
Small Town Joy: From Glam Rock to Hyper-Pop, How Queer Music Shaped the Sound of Scotland by Carrie Marshall
How Does Change Happen? Scenes from the Frontlines of Activism by Sam Gonçalves
Speak Still: Articulating the Silence of Bilingualism by Wing Lam Tong
Clean Up on Aisle Earth: How Technology Drives Climate Action by Tasmin Lockwood

2026

But We Did: Dismantling Colonialist Myths Towards Collective Liberation by Titilayo Farukuoye
Publisher Not Found: A Decade of Disruption, 404 Ink 2016 – 2026 by Heather McDaid and Laura Jones-Rivera

About the Authors

Heather McDaid was the publisher and co-founder of 404 Ink and is the co-founder of the graphic novel development agency One Shot Studios. She has also been Publishing and Campaigns Manager at the Terry Pratchett Estate, Programme Support Officer at Publishing Scotland and Programmer at Paisley Book Festival. She was named a Bookseller Rising Star and spends as much time as she can hanging with her family and raising two little icons.

Laura Jones-Rivera was the publisher and co-founder of 404 Ink and is currently a SGSAH-funded PhD Researcher in small press publishing and diversity at the University of Stirling. She is also Operations Manager at Charco Press and a book typesetter for clients such as Bloomsbury, Cipher Press, Hajar Press and many more. She lives in Edinburgh, Scotland, with her husband.